Table of Contents

Preface

Welcome to *Guide to Writing Quality Individualized Education Programs* (2nd Edition).

We designed this guide for anyone involved in the special education of students with disabilities. It is useful for parents, preservice and inservice education professionals, and others who support families or provide services to these students. We know that many of you regularly serve, or will serve, on teams that provide educational services to students with disabilities, and you will likely be responsible for contributing to the development of Individualized Education Programs (IEPs). This guide will facilitate your collaborative work on these teams.

Our goal is to help you write quality IEPs. Since the IEP is a legal document which guides the education of students with disabilities, it is critical that you have the skills and knowledge to write IEPs that meet the standards of the law. To help you gain a deeper understanding of this process, we have organized this guide with several features:

- Summary of IDEA 2004 in language that is easy to understand

- Sample IEPs of four students with varying disabilities and ages: Tabib, a 1st grade boy with autism; Herbie, a 3rd grade boy with specific learning disabilities; Brittany, an 8th grade girl with severe emotional disturbance; and Isabel, a 20-year-old woman with mental retardation.

- Sample transition plan

- Organization of the IEP process into seven manageable steps

- Explanation, modeling, practice, and feedback for each step as you learn to write an IEP

- Brief procedural summary at the end of each step

- Personal guide, Mr. Mentor, who provides comments, directions, and suggestions as you read and complete each step in the guide

Assumptions behind this guide

In developing this guide we have assumed that you and the rest of the school team have completed the identification, referral, evaluation, and classification processes for your students with disabilities. This guide begins at the point when your team is ready to develop students' IEPs.

Parameters for this guide

This guide does not address planning for students without disabilities who struggle in school. Unless they also have a disability, students whose primary language is not English;

whose learning difficulties are caused by environmental, cultural, or economic disadvantages; or who have not received appropriate instruction are not eligible for special education, and therefore do not need an IEP. These students may be served by other programs.

Legal basis for this guide

Federal law mandates the special education process, so we have structured this guide in accordance with federal law and regulations, and we use terminology from the federal law throughout the text. Individual states must meet the requirements of the federal law, but may also add specific state policies and procedures. You should consult your state and district regulations for their specific policies, procedures, and terminology.

Acknowledgments

We express our gratitude to Jonathan Saltzman for his skills and craft as a typographer. We also thank Sharon Black and Nari Carter for their help with editing, and Virginia Lanigan for her patient support of our efforts in writing this second edition.

—*GSG and TTD*

About the Authors

Gordon S. Gibb, Ph.D., taught students with disabilities in the public schools for 16 years prior to his appointment at Brigham Young University in 1995. As an associate professor in the Department of Counseling Psychology and Special Education, Dr. Gibb prepares teachers to work with students with mild/moderate disabilities and conducts instructional improvement activities in several schools. Dr. Gibb earned his doctorate in special education from the University of Utah in 1994. His research centers on general teacher effectiveness and on language arts instruction for students with disabilities. Dr. Gibb and his wife, Vickie, have four children and live in Pleasant Grove, Utah.

Tina Taylor Dyches, Ed.D., is an associate professor and Director for Special Education Programs in the Department of Counseling Psychology and Special Education at Brigham Young University. Dr. Dyches has worked with individuals with significant disabilities and their families for more than 20 years as a special educator and professor. Her service and research interests include adaptation of families raising children with disabilities, multicultural issues affecting children with autism and their families, children's literature that characterizes individuals with disabilities, and provision of appropriate services to individuals with disabilities. Dr. Dyches lives in Mt. Pleasant, Utah, with her husband, David, and son, Logan.

Introduction: Special Education and the Individualized Education Program

You have no doubt studied the American Civil Rights Movement of the 1950s and 60s, when great strides were made toward eliminating discrimination, and laws were enacted to establish equal rights for all citizens, regardless of their individual differences. But did you know that during this same time many children with disabilities were not allowed to attend American public schools? As recently as the 1970s, students with a variety of disabilities were routinely excluded from public education. Reasons for this discrimination usually had to do with inconvenience, untrained teachers, or fears that other students would be adversely affected by associating with children with disabilities. Fortunately, this all changed when advocates for children and families prevailed upon Congress to establish the Education for All Handicapped Children Act in 1975. This law mandated that all children in the United States have the right to a free and appropriate education at public expense; this mandate is the legal foundation for modern special education. Today the law is referred to as the *Individuals with Disabilities Education Act of 2004* (IDEA).

What is special education?

According to IDEA, special education is defined as follows:

> *Specially designed instruction, at no cost to parents, to meet the unique needs of a student with a disability, including instruction conducted in the classroom, in the home, in hospitals and institutions, and in other settings; and instruction in physical education.* (34 CFR §300.39)

To provide special education, each state must assure that all students ages 3–21 with disabilities who reside in the state have access to these five provisions:

1. **Free Appropriate Public Education.** This is defined as special education and related services that

   - are provided at public expense, under public supervision, and without charge,

   - meet the standards of the state educational agency,

   - include appropriate preschool, elementary school, or secondary school education, and

   - are provided consistent with each student's individualized education program. (34 CFR §300.17)

2. **Appropriate Evaluation.** To serve a student in special education, a school must first conduct an evaluation to determine if the student has a disability, if the disability inhibits progress in the general curriculum, and if special education is needed to meet the student's individual needs. This evaluation must

   - use a variety of assessment tools and strategies to gather relevant functional, developmental, and academic information,

- avoid relying on any single measure or assessment to determine if a student has a disability,

- use technically sound instruments that may assess the relative contribution of cognitive and behavioral factors, in addition to physical or developmental factors,

- be selected and administered with care to avoid racial or cultural discrimination,

- be provided and administered in the language and form most likely to yield accurate information on what the student knows and can do academically, developmentally, and functionally, unless this is not feasible,

- use instruments that are valid and reliable,

- assess the student in all areas of suspected disability, and

- allow for coordination between schools for students who transfer from one district to another in the same academic year. (34 CFR §300.304)

3. **Individualized Education Program.** If the results of the evaluation indicate that a student needs special education, then an individualized education program (IEP) must be developed. The IEP is a written document that includes the following:

- A statement of the student's present levels of academic achievement and functional performance, including

    — how the disability affects the student's involvement and progress in the general education curriculum or, for preschool students, how the disability affects participation in appropriate activities,

    — for students who take alternate assessments aligned with alternate achievement standards, a description of benchmarks or short-term objectives.

- A statement of measurable annual goals, including academic and functional goals, designed to

    — meet the student's needs that result from the disability, enabling the student to be involved in and make progress in the general curriculum, and

    — meet each of the student's other educational needs that result from the disability.

- A description of how the student's progress toward meeting the annual goals will be measured and when periodic reports on the student's progress will be provided.

- A statement of the special education, related services, and supplementary aids and services, based on peer-reviewed research to the extent practicable, to be provided to the student

    — to advance toward attaining the annual goals,

    — to be involved in and make progress in the general education curriculum, and

    — to participate in extracurricular and other nonacademic activities.

- An explanation of the extent, if any, to which the student will not participate with nondisabled students in the regular class and in extracurricular and other nonacademic activities.

- A statement of any individual appropriate accommodations that are necessary to measure the academic achievement and functional performance of the student on state and district-wide assessments, and if the IEP Team determines that the student shall take an alternate assessment, explanations of

   — why the student cannot participate in the regular assessment, and

   — which alternate assessment has been selected as appropriate for the student.

- The projected date for the beginning of the IEP and the anticipated frequency, location, and duration of the services and modifications.

- Beginning not later than the first IEP to be in effect when the student is 16, and updated annually thereafter,

   — appropriate measurable post-secondary goals based upon age-appropriate transition assessments related to training, education, employment, and, where appropriate, independent living skills,

   — the transition services, including courses of study, needed to assist the student in reaching those goals, and

   — beginning not later than one year before the student reaches the age of majority under state law, a statement that the student has been informed of the rights that will transfer to him or her on reaching the age of majority. (CFR §300.320)

4. **Least Restrictive Environment.** This means that to the maximum extent appropriate students with disabilities, including students in public or private institutions or other care facilities, are educated with students without disabilities, and special classes, separate schooling, or other removal of students with disabilities from the regular educational environment occurs only when the nature or severity of a student's disability is such that education in regular classes with the use of supplementary aids and services cannot be achieved satisfactorily. (34 CFR §300.114)

5. **Procedural Safeguards.** Schools must establish and maintain procedures to ensure that students with disabilities and their parents are guaranteed procedural safeguards as a free appropriate public education is provided. Written notice of the procedural safeguards must be in the native language of the parents, unless use of this language is clearly not feasible, and documents must be written in an easily understandable style. The notice must include a full explanation of the following safeguards:

- Parents may present information from an independent educational evaluation to be considered in determining the existence of a disability and/or designating the contents of the IEP.

- Parents must be provided with written notice before any action is taken with regard to the education of their child with a disability.

- Parents must provide written consent before any action is taken with regard to the education of their child with a disability.

- Parents have access to their child's educational records.

- Parents have the opportunity to present and participate in resolving complaints.

- Parents have the right to an explanation of the student's placement pending a due process hearing.
- Parents should receive an explanation of procedures for students who are subject to placement in an interim alternative educational setting.
- Parents should be provided an explanation of the requirements for unilateral placement they may make of students in private schools at public expense.
- Parents should receive an explanation of the procedures for due process hearings.
- State-level appeals should be explained to parents.
- Procedures for civil actions should be explained to parents.
- Attorney's fees should be discussed with parents. (34 CFR §300.500-536)

These five principles have been part of special education since the first law was passed in 1975. The requirements for each principle have been altered somewhat in subsequent reauthorizations of IDEA, but the basic framework of special education in the United States has remained the same.

How does the special education process begin?

The special education process begins with a referral by parents or a teacher for evaluation to determine if a child has a disability. When a disability is evident before or after a child is born or during the preschool years, parents make the referral. However, most disabilities are identified when a student does not achieve as expected in school. When this is the case, the classroom teacher must provide evidence of the student's participation in scientific, research-based intervention(s) to address the student's individual needs, and provide data about the effects of the intervention(s) on the student's achievement. If the interventions are unsuccessful at meeting the student's needs, the teacher can initiate a referral to determine if the student has a disability. If appropriate assessment indicates that the student has a disability and is eligible for special education services, then an IEP is developed.

What is the role of the IEP in special education?

The IEP is a legal document with two essential roles. First, it is the individualized component of special education planning, defining what *appropriate* means in each student's free appropriate public education. The IEP describes a student's special education program for one year, including goals for improvement and ways the school will help the student achieve the goals. The emphasis is on the student making progress in the general curriculum and participating in extracurricular activities of an appropriate nature and extent. Students with disabilities are not to be isolated and separated from their peers, but are to take part in school as other students do. The IEP might be viewed as a personal roadmap for a student's education.

Second, the IEP serves as a communication tool between parents and teachers regarding the student's educational growth and achievement. When parents and teachers both know the goals for student improvement, they have common reference points for discussion and decisions.

Who needs an IEP?

Any student between the ages of 3 and 21 who is classified with a disability, as described in IDEA, and who receives special education services must have a current IEP. IDEA disability classifications are discussed in Step 4.

Are IEPs created for children with disabilities younger than age 3 or older than 21?

No. Special education is provided for infants and toddlers to age 3 who have been diagnosed with disabilities or developmental delays, but such interventions are based on an *Individualized Family Service Plan* (IFSP) instead of an IEP. The IFSP focuses not only on the child, but also on the concerns, needs, and resources of the family. The IFSP facilitates the child's transition to preschool or other services or discontinues special education services that are no longer needed.

Adults with disabilities are not eligible for special education services after their 22nd birthday; therefore, these individuals do not have IEPs. From this age, individuals who still need services must depend on family or community support or on government agencies to meet their needs. Unfortunately, there is no guarantee that services will be available for all adults who need them. Availability of services for adults with disabilities varies greatly across the United States.

Who develops the IEP?

The IEP is developed by a team that meets and discusses relevant information about the student's strengths and needs. IDEA states that the IEP team must consist of these members:

- The parents of the student with a disability
- At least one regular education teacher of the student if the student is or may be participating in the regular class
- At least one special education teacher or one special education provider
- A representative of the local education agency (LEA) who is qualified to provide or supervise the provision of special education for the student, is knowledgeable about the general education curriculum, and is knowledgeable about the availability of resources
- An individual who can interpret evaluation results, possibly one of those already mentioned on this list
- At the discretion of the parent or school, other individuals who have knowledge or special expertise regarding the student
- Whenever appropriate, the student with a disability. (34 CFR §300.321)

Please remember that each member of the IEP team contributes unique and essential information. Parents may be intimidated by the IEP process or may feel less qualified than the professionals on the team; however, parents know their children better than anyone else does. Parental input must be sought and valued throughout the IEP process.

Who has access to the IEP?

Parents and authorized school and district personnel may access a student's IEP and other personally identifiable education records. IDEA uses the *Federal Education Right to Privacy Act* (FERPA) definition of *education records.* IDEA requires schools to maintain a publicly visible record of access on which authorized people must record their name, position, date, and reason for accessing these confidential materials. Parents may request copies of a student's IEP and other confidential information, as defined by FERPA.

The law's careful description of access rights has two purposes: (1) it defines who can see a student's personally identifiable information, and (2) it informs schools and parents that this information is *confidential,* meaning that unauthorized people do not have access to it. For IEP team members, strict confidentiality is required regarding students served by special education. Team members may not disclose confidential information to others, spoken or written, in or out of school.

Perhaps you have heard the story of the teacher who was complaining to a friend in line at the grocery store about the trials of working with a particular student in special education. Of course, the next person in line was the student's mother, who promptly reported the teacher's breach of confidentiality to the school and district. The lesson demonstrated by this episode is that teachers must share confidential information only with authorized people at appropriate times and in appropriate settings.

What happens during an IEP meeting?

Usually the team members meet around a table in a room or office where confidential information can be shared. One of the school professionals conducts the meeting and introduces the participants. If an IEP is currently in place, then the team evaluates the student's progress toward or achievement of the previous annual goals. The team members then discuss and write the new IEP. The format of IEP meetings may vary from school to school and district to district, but the general procedures are the same.

Writing IEPs improves with practice, but a set of steps is useful to beginners when completing this important process. All schools have either paper forms or IEP software which should include the required components. We have been surprised that many of the IEPs we have seen are formatted to start at the wrong place in the process: They begin with what services the student will receive instead of how the student is currently performing in school. In this case, teams are inclined to decide special education placement and services before describing and discussing the student's goals for improvement—a classic case of the cart before the horse.

What steps does the team follow to develop an IEP?

We have outlined seven steps that lead your team through the process of developing quality IEPs.

Describe the student's present levels of academic achievement and functional performance.

 Write measurable annual goals.

 Measure and report student progress.

 State the services needed to achieve annual goals.

 Explain the extent, if any, to which the student will not participate with nondisabled students in the regular class and in extracurricular and other nonacademic activities.

 Explain accommodations necessary to measure academic achievement and functional performance on state and district-wide assessments.

 Complete a transition plan for students aged 16 and older.

When these steps are completed, all IEP team members confirm their participation in the meeting by signing and dating the IEP.

How do I complete each of the steps in the IEP process?

The completion process is what you will learn and practice with this guide. As you go along you will find a rationale and explanation for each of the steps so that you can complete the process knowledgeably and professionally. You will also see examples from four case studies of students with disabilities and, where appropriate, counterexamples to guide your learning and to help you discriminate between correct and incorrect procedures. Then you will practice each of the steps to check your understanding. As you complete each self-check exercise, you can compare your answers with our suggested answers in the Appendix.

Reference

U.S. Department of Education Assistance to States for the Education of Children With Disabilities and Preschool Grants for Children With Disabilities; Final Rule, 34 CFR Parts 300 and 301 (2006). Available at: www.ed.gov/policy/speced/guid/idea/idea2004.html#law

YOU ARE READY TO GO! **ENJOY** YOUR LEARNING, AND MAY YOU FIND **SUCCESS** AND **FULFILLMENT** AS YOU PLAN FOR THESE MARVELOUS CHILDREN.

Meet Our Students

We have provided four cases to guide our explanation of the steps in writing quality IEPs. Read about Herbie, Brittany, Tabib, and Isabel, and then read over their IEPs. We will refer to these students throughout the book.

HERBIE MAXWELL

Herbie Maxwell is an eight-year-old Caucasian boy with specific learning disabilities attending Mrs. Foreman's 3rd-grade class at Rockland Elementary School.

Family and Cultural Background

Herbie lives with his mother, step-father, and two younger half-sisters in a rented home. His step-father works as a farm mechanic and his mother is a part-time secretary at the junior high school. Both parents were raised in the area and family recreation is mainly local camping and fishing. His mother occasionally expresses a desire to "take the kids somewhere fun, like Disneyland," but this has not been financially possible. Herbie would like to be in 4-H when he is older but his family does not own land and the cost of raising a calf or foal for a livestock project seems prohibitive at this time. Neither parent attended college, but they support the school system and expect their children to graduate from high school. Herbie speaks English at home and school.

Prior School Experience

Herbie struggled with beginning reading and math concepts in first grade and by second grade his teacher realized that he was behind the average learning curve. The teacher held two conferences with Herbie's parents to discuss her concerns. They decided that the teacher would send home practice work with Herbie and that his parents would work with him each evening. This did not help much because Herbie often neglected to bring the work home or his parents were too tired or too busy to sit down with him. By the end of second grade Herbie was significantly behind grade level in basic reading and math skills.

By early October of his third-grade year Mrs. Foreman realized that Herbie was not progressing even though he was working hard in the classroom. She moved Herbie's seat to the front of the room near her desk and placed him with higher-achieving peers for group work. Herbie enjoyed the teacher's attention, but his basic skills did not improve. Mrs. Foreman discussed her concerns with the special education teacher and finally referred Herbie for special education assessment during the first week of November.

Special education assessment data were analyzed by the Child Study Team which determined that Herbie has specific learning disabilities in reading and math. In addition, his history of failure seemed to discourage him from trying to learn. Provision of special education services were directed toward skill remediation and academic success.

Current Schooling

Rockland Elementary serves students in a rural mining and farming community in which employment is stable but low-paying and offers little opportunity for advancement in career or salary. The school enrolls 172 students in grades K–6, of which 84% are Caucasian, 13% Hispanic, 2% American Indian, and 1% Asian. In addition, 17% of Rockland's students are served by special education and 57% are economically disadvantaged.

Relevant Instructional and Behavioral Information

Herbie knows the letter names and sounds and can read 20 first-grade nonsense word sounds correct in one minute, compared to nondisabled peers who read 50 or more correct per minute. In third grade he reads 8 words correct per minute on first-grade oral reading passages, but should have been reading 40 or more by the end of first grade. He cannot answer literal or inferential reading comprehension questions from first grade passages. He cannot read second or third grade passages.

Herbie can count to 50, count objects to 50, recognize and write numerals 0–9, and group objects in sets. He recognizes a line, square, and circle, but not a rectangle or triangle. He cannot add or subtract 2 digit by 1 digit problems without regrouping and has not attempted multiplication. His teachers have used manipulative objects to teach adding and subtracting but only in cooperative learning groups. Herbie has not received individual explicit instruction in math skills.

Herbie does not exhibit disruptive behaviors and always speaks respectfully to the teacher, as he has been taught at home. However, he seldom engages in group or independent work, and has started laying his head on the desk when he should be working. He responds well to stories read by the teacher, but seems very discouraged about learning to read. He plays well with his peers at recess and eats with a group of friends in the cafeteria.

INDIVIDUALIZED EDUCATION PROGRAM

Student *Herbie Maxwell*   Birth date *7/30*   IEP Date *12/16*

School *Rockland Elementary*   Grade *3*   Classification *Specific learning disabilities*

Present Levels of Academic Achievement and Functional Performance

Preschool students: Describe how the disability affects the student's participation in appropriate activities.

School-age students: Describe how the disability affects the student's involvement and progress in the general curriculum.

Herbie knows letter names and sounds, and reads 20 1st-grade nonsense word sounds correct in one minute. He reads 1st-grade oral reading passages at 8 words correct per minute. He cannot answer literal or inferential reading comprehension questions from first grade passages. He cannot read second or third grade passages.

Herbie can count to 50, count objects to 50, recognize and write numerals 0–9, and group objects in sets. He recognizes a line, square, and circle, but not a rectangle or triangle. He cannot add or subtract 2 digit by 1 digit problems without regrouping, and has not attempted multiplication. These difficulties in reading and math inhibit his progress in the general curriculum.

Measurable Annual Goals

1. *Given a 150 word 2.5 grade level reading passage, Herbie will orally read 68 or more words correctly in one minute with 95% accuracy, 3/3 consecutive trials.*

Student's progress toward goal measured by: ☒ Curriculum-based Measures ☐ Behavior Observation
☐ Skills Checklist ☐ Work Sample ☐ Test Results ☐ Other

2. *Given a 150 word 2.5 grade level reading passage, Herbie will orally read the passage and correctly answer 4/5 literal and inferential comprehension questions, 2/2 consecutive trials.*

Student's progress toward goal measured by: ☒ Curriculum-based Measures ☐ Behavior Observation
☐ Skills Checklist ☐ Work Sample ☐ Test Results ☐ Other

3. *Given a sheet of geometric shapes Herbie will correctly mark a rectangle, triangle, cube, and cylinder, 2/2 consecutive trials over two weeks.*

Student's progress toward goal measured by: ☒ Curriculum-based Measures ☐ Behavior Observation
☐ Skills Checklist ☐ Work Sample ☐ Test Results ☐ Other

4. *When directed by the teacher, Herbie will rote count and write numerals to 120 with no errors, 3/3 trials over 3 consecutive weeks.*

Student's progress toward goal measured by: ☒ Curriculum-based Measures ☐ Behavior Observation
☒ Skills Checklist ☐ Work Sample ☐ Test Results ☐ Other

5. *Given 10 addition and 10 subtraction problems, 3 digit by 3 digit with regrouping, Herbie will solve and write 9/10 answers correctly, 2/2 consecutive trials.*

Student's progress toward goal measured by: ☒ Curriculum-based Measures ☐ Behavior Observation
☐ Skills Checklist ☐ Work Sample ☐ Test Results ☐ Other

Services to Achieve Annual Goals and Advance in General Curriculum

Special Education Services   R = *Regular class* S = *Special class* O = *Other* D = *Daily* W = *Weekly* M = *Monthly*

Service	Location	Time	Frequency	Begin date	Duration
Specially designed instruction	R Ⓢ O:	*275 min*	D Ⓦ M	*12/16*	①yr O:

Related Services to Benefit from Special Education

Service	Location	Time	Frequency	Begin date	Duration
	R S O:		D W M		1 yr O:

Program Modifications and/or Supplementary Aids and Services in Regular Classes

Modifications/Personnel Support	Frequency	Supplementary Aids and Services	Frequency
	D W M	*Tests written at grade 1 reading level*	D Ⓦ M

Applicable Special Factors

Factor	Not Needed	In IEP
Positive behavior instruction and support when behavior impedes learning of student or others	✔	
Language needs for student with limited English proficiency	✔	
Braille instruction for student who is blind or visually impaired	✔	
Communication and/or language services for student who is deaf, hard of hearing, or has other communication needs	✔	
Assistive technology devices or services	✔	

Participation in Regular Class, Extracurricular and Nonacademic Activities

The student will participate in the regular class, extracurricular and nonacademic activities except as noted above and listed here: ☐ _____

Schedule for Written IEP Progress Reports to Parents

☐ Weekly   ☐ Bi-weekly   ⎤ *via* ⎡ ☐ Progress report   ☒ Report card
☐ Monthly   ☒ Quarterly   ⎦   ⎣ ☐ Home note   ☐ Parent Conference

Transition Plan

Complete and attach for students age 16 and older.

Participation in State and District Assessments

Participation Codes

S	Standard administration	No accommodations or modifications
A	Participate with accommodations	Does not invalidate, alter, or lower standard
M	Participate with modifications	Invalidates, alters, or lowers standard
AA	Participate using alternate assessment: ☐ Out-of-level CRT ☐ State alternate assessment	Aligned more closely with alternate curriculum than general education curriculum

State and District Assessment Matrix   Enter appropriate participation code for each applicable assessment.

Grade	Kindergarten Pretest	Kindergarten Posttest	State Criterion Referenced Math	State Criterion Referenced Language Arts	State Criterion Referenced Science	Iowa Test of Basic Skills	National Assessment Educational Progress
K							
1							
2							
3			A	S	A	A	A
4							
5							
6							
7							
8							
9							
10							
11							
12							

Accommodations and Modifications   List specific accommodations and modifications for assessments.

Teacher reads test to student, except for reading tests or subtests.

Alternate Assessment

State why student cannot participate in regular assessment:

State why selected alternate assessment is appropriate:

Student *Herbie Maxwell*   Date   *12/16*

IEP Team Participants

SIGMUND MAXWELL   Parent

Ruth McCausland   LEA Representative

Herbie Maxwell   Student

Sue Ann Foreman   Regular Class Teacher

Tawny Bright   Special Education Teacher

     School Psychologist

If parent signature missing, provide copy of IEP and Procedural Safeguards and check below:

☐ Did not attend (document efforts to involve parent)

☐ Via telephone

☐ Other

Comments

BRITTANY HUANG

Brittany Huang is a 13-year-old eighth-grade girl with severe emotional disturbance attending Emerald Hills Middle School.

Family and Cultural Background

Brittany and her 10-year-old sister live with their parents in a wealthy suburban area populated by business and medical professionals. Mr. and Mrs. Huang emigrated from southern China as children and grew up together in a mostly non-English-speaking immigrant Chinese neighborhood where day labor was the common employment. Their parents worked very hard to provide every educational opportunity for their children. As a result, both Mr. and Mrs. Huang are now successful physicians. Their practices are very demanding, however, so the girls are often home alone until 7:00 or 8:00 o'clock in the evening. The family lives in a very nice house and the parents enjoy providing their children with gifts, entertainment, and the latest fashions. The girls associate with school and neighborhood friends who enjoy the same advantages.

Prior School Experience

Brittany seemed to be an average student through 5th-grade but during 6th-grade her interest in school declined. She became selective in her compliance with teacher requests—"moody" was the term her teacher used—and was increasingly defiant at home. She transformed from a friendly and likable child to a demanding and disagreeable girl who alienated most of the adults in her life as well as many of her friends. In April, her 6th-grade teacher met with the Huangs to discuss her concerns. Mr. and Mrs. Huang also noticed the changes, but thought Brittany was most likely in the throes of early adolescence. The teacher remarked that Brittany's behavior seemed different than other students she could remember, and she wondered aloud if there was more to the situation. Brittany's school achievement declined rapidly, but nothing further was accomplished before school ended in June.

One day in late July, Mrs. Huang received a disturbing phone call during which her younger daughter sobbed out a story about Brittany screaming and crying in her room. Brittany would not talk on the phone so Mrs. Huang drove home to investigate. With patient listening and gentle coaxing, Brittany revealed that she hates herself and everyone else, and she "just can't stand it anymore." She could not give a specific reason for her feelings, but her recent history and current emotional state convinced Mrs. Huang that Brittany needed professional help. Following three visits to a clinical psychologist, Brittany was diagnosed with severe anger and mood disorders. The psychologist recommended that the Huangs refer Brittany for special education so she could receive the help she needed at school. As a result, Brittany was classified with severe emotional disturbance in late November of 7th grade.

Current Schooling

Emerald Hills Middle School serves 310 seventh graders and 325 eighth graders, of which 82% are Caucasian, 14% are Asian, and 4% are African American. The school uses a teaming system in which English, social studies, and science teachers share cohorts of students and meet in team meetings once each week. Expectations for success are high, and families and teachers anticipate that most students will go on to attend college and graduate school.

Relevant Instructional and Behavioral Information

Brittany is near grade level in basic academic achievement. She reads and comprehends at the 7.0 grade equivalent level, and her math reasoning skills are also at the 7.5 grade equivalent level. She does not work well independently, often yelling and exhibiting other defiant behavior when asked to complete work on her own; and she does not ask the teacher for assistance when she has difficulty with assignments. When given a variable-time delayed redirection to begin work, she pushes her desktop materials to the floor and puts her head down. She currently attends a resource study skills class for one period per day, during which the teacher works with Brittany to develop replacement behaviors to eliminate her outbursts and her refusal to work. The resource teacher reinforces the desired behaviors while co-teaching in Brittany's regular English and social studies classes.

INDIVIDUALIZED EDUCATION PROGRAM

Student _Brittany Huang_   Birth date _6/21_   IEP Date _11/23_

School _Emerald Hills Middle_   Grade _8_   Classification _Severe emotional disturbance_

Present Levels of Academic Achievement and Functional Performance

Preschool students: Describe how the disability affects the student's participation in appropriate activities.

School-age students: Describe how the disability affects the student's involvement and progress in the general curriculum.

Brittany reads and comprehends at the 7.0 grade equivalent level, writes accurate sentences and paragraphs, and her math reasoning skills are at the 7.5 grade equivalent level. When directed by the teacher to work independently, she yells defiantly and refuses to begin work 80% of observed instances across settings. When given a variable-time delayed redirection to begin work, she pushes her desktop materials to the floor and puts her head down, 80% of observed instances. She does not ask the teacher for assistance when she does not understand the assignment. Brittany's behaviors inhibit her functional performance and achievement in the general curriculum.

Measurable Annual Goals

1. _When directed by the teacher to begin assignments, Brittany will leave her materials on her desk, 100% of instances in each class over a 4-week period._

Student's progress toward goal measured by: ☐ Curriculum-based Measures ☒ Behavior Observation
☐ Skills Checklist ☐ Work Sample ☐ Test Results ☐ Other _____

2. _When directed by the teacher to work independently, Brittany will quietly begin the assignment within 10 seconds, 90% of instances in each of her classes over a 4-week period._

Student's progress toward goal measured by: ☐ Curriculum-based Measures ☒ Behavior Observation
☐ Skills Checklist ☐ Work Sample ☐ Test Results ☐ Other _____

3. _When needing assistance from the teacher to complete an assignment, Brittany will raise her hand, ask for assistance when called on, and wait for the teacher to assist her, 90% of instances in each class over a 6-week period._

Student's progress toward goal measured by: ☐ Curriculum-based Measures ☒ Behavior Observation
☐ Skills Checklist ☐ Work Sample ☐ Test Results ☐ Other _____

4. _____

Student's progress toward goal measured by: ☐ Curriculum-based Measures ☐ Behavior Observation
☐ Skills Checklist ☐ Work Sample ☐ Test Results ☐ Other _____

5. _____

Student's progress toward goal measured by: ☐ Curriculum-based Measures ☐ Behavior Observation
☐ Skills Checklist ☐ Work Sample ☐ Test Results ☐ Other _____

Services to Achieve Annual Goals and Advance in General Curriculum

Special Education Services   R = *Regular class* S = *Special class* O = *Other* D = *Daily* W = *Weekly* M = *Monthly*

Service	Location	Time	Frequency	Begin date	Duration
Specially designed instruction	(R)(S) O:	*150 min*	(D) W M	*11/23*	(1 yr) O:

Related Services to Benefit from Special Education

Service	Location	Time	Frequency	Begin date	Duration
Counseling	R S (O:) *Office*	*30 min*	D (W) M	*11/23*	(1 yr) O:

Program Modifications and/or Supplementary Aids and Services in Regular Classes

Modifications/Personnel Support	Frequency	Supplementary Aids and Services	Frequency
	D W M		D W M

Applicable Special Factors

Factor	Not Needed	In IEP
Positive behavior instruction and support when behavior impedes learning of student or others		✔
Language needs for student with limited English proficiency	✔	
Braille instruction for student who is blind or visually impaired	✔	
Communication and/or language services for student who is deaf, hard of hearing, or has other communication needs	✔	
Assistive technology devices or services	✔	

Participation in Regular Class, Extracurricular and Nonacademic Activities

The student will participate in the regular class, extracurricular and nonacademic activities except as noted above and listed here: ☐ _____

Schedule for Written IEP Progress Reports to Parents

☐ Weekly   ☐ Bi-weekly ⎤ *via* ⎡ ☒ Progress report   ☒ Report card
☐ Monthly   ☒ Quarterly ⎦   ⎣ ☐ Home note   ☐ Parent Conference

Transition Plan

Complete and attach for students age 16 and older.

Participation in State and District Assessments

Participation Codes

S	Standard administration	No accommodations or modifications
A	Participate with accommodations	Does not invalidate, alter, or lower standard
M	Participate with modifications	Invalidates, alters, or lowers standard
AA	Participate using alternate assessment: ☐ Out-of-level CRT ☐ State alternate assessment	Aligned more closely with alternate curriculum than general education curriculum

State and District Assessment Matrix   Enter appropriate participation code for each applicable assessment.

Grade	Kindergarten Pretest	Kindergarten Posttest	State Criterion Referenced Math	State Criterion Referenced Language Arts	State Criterion Referenced Science	Iowa Test of Basic Skills	National Assessment Educational Progress
K							
1							
2							
3							
4							
5							
6							
7							
8			S	S	S	S	S
9							
10							
11							
12							

Accommodations and Modifications   List specific accommodations and modifications for assessments.

_____

_____

_____

_____

Alternate Assessment

State why student cannot participate in regular assessment: _____

_____

_____

State why selected alternate assessment is appropriate: _____

_____

_____

_____

Student _Brittany Huang_   Date _11/23_

IEP Team Participants

Iwei Huang	Parent
Melvin Grubner	LEA Representative
Brittany Huang	Student
Giselle LaFontaine	Regular Class Teacher
Carlotta Rigutto	Special Education Teacher
Mercy Sack-Smith	School Psychologist

If parent signature missing, provide copy of IEP and Procedural Safeguards and check below:

☐ Did not attend (document efforts to involve parent)

☐ Via telephone

☐ Other _____

Comments

TABIB WILSON

Tabib Wilson is a six-year-old African American boy diagnosed with autism.

Family and Cultural Background

Tabib lives at home with an 8-year-old sister, a 2-year-old brother, his mom and dad, and his maternal grandmother. Mr. Wilson works as a manager at the local safe company and Mrs. Wilson works part time as a nurse. Tabib's grandmother tends the younger brother while his parents are working. They are African American and have strong family, cultural, and religious traditions. Tabib has been accepted by his church and neighborhood, and they are actively engaged in learning how to effectively integrate Tabib into the community.

Prior School Experience

Mrs. Wilson noticed Tabib's unusual development when he was two years old and wondered if he might have autism. While at times he appeared to be unusually bright, he often acted like he was deaf, or was "in his own world." After visiting with several medical and psychological professionals, his diagnosis was confirmed.

Tabib was diagnosed as having autism when he was three years old. He attended a preschool for students with Autism Spectrum Disorders (ASD) for two years, and last year he attended Kindergarten at Jefferson Elementary in a class for students with developmental delays.

Current Schooling

Tabib is currently in the 1st grade in his neighborhood school, Jefferson Elementary. This school has 576 students with one principal and 26 teachers. The current first grade at Jefferson Elementary consists of 77 students. Of these students, 84% (65) are white; 12% (9) are Hispanic; 4% (3) are African American; 9% (7) have limited English proficiency; and 17% (13) have disabilities. Almost one-third (32%) of the students in the school are eligible for free/reduced lunch.

Tabib's teacher, Ms. Burton, teaches students in the "Small Group Classroom" program. This is a special education program for students in the 1st–3rd grades who require a high teacher-to-student ratio in order to access the general curriculum and to function independently in society. Seven other students attend this classroom, many of whom have ASD. Ms. Burton is assisted by two full-time paraeducators.

Ms. Burton reports that Tabib's curriculum is designed to promote effective communication, positive social skills, and a reduction of restrictive routines. However, his curriculum is tied to the general curriculum and Tabib is approaching grade level work in some areas of math and physical education. Tabib learns best when he is given realistic expectations, clear visual and verbal directions, and standard functional routines.

Relevant Instructional and Behavioral Information

Academic. Recent developmental testing in a 1:1 situation with Ms. Burton, the special educator, indicates that Tabib's math skills are at a 5–3 age level in math (e.g., recognizing patterns with one or two attributes, identifying simple geometric shapes). His reading skills are at a 5–6 age level. He can match uppercase and lowercase letters, visually discriminate between three symbols, and select 20 pictures on his communication device. His writing skills are below a 5–3 age level. He can trace 12 letters, but is unable to print letters or words independently. In other areas tested, Tabib demonstrates skills at the 3–4 year old level.

Social. Tabib is a happy child and can entertain himself for long periods of time with water, strings, Disney DVDs, and Legos. He does not initiate play with his peers, and only engages in parallel play if the other children are playing with toys that interest him. Tabib often takes toys from his friends rather than asking for a turn (on average 6 times per day).

Communication. Tabib uses various means to communicate. He has a limited vocabulary of five spoken words (i.e., "mom," "no," "yeah," "water," "Lego"). He can communicate many of his wants and needs in sentence format by using an electronic communication device (e.g., "I want" + "DVD"). He has a 20-word vocabulary using this device. He can consistently sign 10 basic words (e.g., "more," "want," "candy," "drink," "play"). Tabib's mother reports that he appears to understand most of what is communicated directly to him. Tabib does not currently use social greetings or communicate with his peers.

Behavior. When prevented from participating in desired activities, or when he is told "no," Tabib often screams and bites his wrist. He has difficulty transitioning from one activity to another, particularly if he is actively engaged with the current activity. These transitions have been made easier for him as his teachers and parents have created a daily visual schedule for him to follow. However, he still screams and bites his wrist an average of 10 times per day when asked to change activities. Tabib also gets upset when in noisy or crowded areas. While he used to hit and scratch others when in such environments, he now just covers his ears and runs out of the area. This creates difficulties for his teachers and his parents, who need to leave the other children and follow Tabib immediately so that he does not encounter dangerous situations (e.g., running out in the street).

Functional Life Skills. Tabib can undress dress himself independently, but he needs verbal prompts to select his clothing and cannot fasten zippers, snaps, or buttons. He resists physical prompts to fasten his clothes.

INDIVIDUALIZED EDUCATION PROGRAM

Student *Tabib Wilson*   Birth date *Aug. 10*   IEP Date *Sept. 15*

School *Jefferson Elementary*   Grade *1st*   Classification *Autism*

Present Levels of Academic Achievement and Functional Performance

Preschool students: Describe how the disability affects the student's participation in appropriate activities.

School-age students: Describe how the disability affects the student's involvement and progress in the general curriculum.

MATH: *According to the State Alternate Assessment (given Sept. 10–13), Tabib is approaching grade level work in some areas of math (e.g., recognizing patterns, identifying simple geometric shapes). However, on average, his math skills are at a 5–3 age level (he can give "one more," give "just one," count to 4 by pointing to objects and point to numbers to five).*

LANGUAGE ARTS: *Tabib's reading skills are at a 5–6 age level (he can match uppercase and lowercase letters, visually discriminate between three symbols, and select 20 pictures on his communication device). His writing skills are below a 5–3 age level (he is able to trace 12 letters, but is unable to print letters or words independently).*

SOCIAL: *Tabib entertains himself for long periods of time, but does not initiate play with his peers, and he only plays alongside others when they have toys that are interesting to him—he often takes those toys rather than asking for a turn (on average 6 times per day). Tabib's social skills hinder his progress in the general curriculum.*

COMMUNICATION: *Tabib communicates with 5 spoken words ("mom," "no," "yeah," "water," "Lego"), and uses an electronic communication device to communicate wants and needs (20-word vocabulary). He also signs 10 basic words. He does not currently use social greetings or communicate with peers. Tabib's limited communication skills inhibit his ability to meet all of the standards of the general curriculum, due to his need for intense, systematic instruction.*

BEHAVIOR: *When thwarted from doing what he wants to do or when transitioning to a different activity, Tabib screams and bites his wrist on average 10 times per day. Tabib is extremely sensitive to noise and crowds of people; in these situations, he often covers his ears and runs out of the area. These behaviors affect his rate of learning the general curriculum.*

FUNCTIONAL LIFE SKILLS: *Tabib can undress dress himself independently, but he needs verbal prompts to select his clothing and cannot fasten zippers, snaps, or buttons. He resists physical prompts to fasten his clothes. These skill deficits are most appropriately addressed with an alternate curriculum.*

Measurable Annual Goals

1. **MATH:** *When assessed on the State Alternate Assessment at the end of the school year, Tabib will increase his math skills to a 6-year-old level in 80% of the sub-domains.*

Benchmarks/Short-term Objectives

a. *When given up to 30 objects to count, Tabib will use one-to-one counting to count the objects (using sign language, communication device, or verbally) with at least 80% accuracy, with at least 3 different types of objects, and maintain for 3 weeks.*

b. *When asked to count as high as he can, Tabib will rote count (using sign language, communication device, or verbally) to 30, with no mistakes, across 3 different conditions, and maintain for 3 weeks.*

c. When asked to identify numbers (0–30), Tabib will point to the correct number with at least 80% accuracy, under 3 different conditions and maintain for 3 weeks.

d. When asked to match the quantity of objects with the numerical symbol (up to 10), Tabib will place the numerical symbol next to the correct number of objects, with at least 80% accuracy, under 3 different conditions, and maintain for 3 weeks.

Student's progress toward goal measured by: ☒ Curriculum-based Measures ☐ Behavior Observation ☐ Skills Checklist ☐ Work Sample ☐ Test Results ☐ Other

2. **LANGUAGE ARTS:** *When assessed on the State Alternate Assessment at the end of the school year, Tabib will increase his reading and writing skills to a 6–3 age level in 80% of the sub-domains.*

Benchmarks/Short-term Objectives

a. When asked to point to uppercase or lowercase letters of the alphabet, Tabib will correctly point to the designated letter with no more than 5 mistakes, with at least 3 different typefonts and maintain for 4 weeks.

b. When presented with 10 pre-primer functional words, Tabib will point to a picture representing each written word, with at least 80% accuracy, using various pictures and typefonts, and maintain for at least 4 weeks.

c. When given 32 new pictures on his communication device, Tabib will activate each picture accurately to provide a comment, over at least 3 times of the day and maintain for at least 4 weeks.

d. When given a visual model of basic words (e.g., first/last name, reading vocabulary), Tabib will copy the words on his paper with at least 80% correct formation, at least 3 times of the day and maintain for at least 4 weeks.

Student's progress toward goal measured by: ☒ Curriculum-based Measures ☐ Behavior Observation ☐ Skills Checklist ☐ Work Sample ☐ Test Results ☐ Other

3. **SOCIAL:** *When other children are playing, Tabib will point to the toy he wants to play with and sign (or activate his communication device) "play," without taking the toy from the child, at least 80% of the time, with at least 3 different toys and in 3 different settings (free time, recess, structured play time), and maintain for 3 weeks.*

Benchmarks/Short-term Objectives

a. In 10 weeks, when children are playing, Tabib will point to the toy he wants to play with and sign or point to "play" with a **full physical prompt,** without taking the toy from the child, at least 80% of the time, with at least 3 different toys and in 3 different settings (free time, recess, structured play time) and maintain for 3 weeks.

b. In 20 weeks, when children are playing, Tabib will point to the toy he wants to play with and sign or point to "play" with a **partial physical prompt,** without taking the toy from the child, at least 80% of the time, with at least 3 different toys and in 3 different settings (free time, recess, structured play time), and maintain for 3 weeks.

c. In 30 weeks, when children are playing, Tabib will point to the toy he wants to play with and sign or point to "play" with a **teacher model,** without taking the toy from the child, at least 80% of the time, with at least 3 different toys and in 3 different settings (free time, recess, structured play time), and maintain for 3 weeks.

Student's progress toward goal measured by: ☐ Curriculum-based Measures ☒ Behavior Observation ☒ Skills Checklist ☐ Work Sample ☐ Test Results ☐ Other

4. **COMMUNICATION:** *When approached by someone who wants to engage in conversation, Tabib will use speech, sign language, or his communication device to make a social greeting and engage in a 1-minute conversation, at least 80% of observed occurrences, with at least 3 different people in 3 different settings, and maintain for 6 weeks.*

Benchmarks/Short-term Objectives

a. *When approached by someone, Tabib will* **wave "hi"** *to the person, at least 80% of observed occurrences, with at least 3 different people in 3 different settings, and maintain for 3 weeks.*

b. *After exchanging greetings with someone, Tabib will* **ask questions and respond** *to the person's questions for 1 minute (using speech, sign language, or his communication device), at least 80% of observed occurrences, with at least 3 different people in 3 different settings, and maintain for 3 weeks.*

Student's progress toward goal measured by: ☐ Curriculum-based Measures ☐ Behavior Observation ☒ Skills Checklist ☐ Work Sample ☐ Test Results ☐ Other _____

5. **BEHAVIOR:** *When asked to stop an activity or to change activities and presented with a visual schedule of the upcoming activity, Tabib will take the visual schedule to the next activity, with zero occurrences of screaming or biting his wrist, over three different conditions and maintain for 4 weeks.*

Benchmarks/Short-term Objectives

a. *When asked to stop an activity or to change activities and presented with a visual schedule of the upcoming activity, Tabib will take the visual schedule to the next activity, with* **fewer than 6** *occurrences of screaming or biting his wrist, over three different conditions and maintain for 2 weeks.*

b. *When asked to stop an activity or to change activities and presented with a visual schedule of the upcoming activity, Tabib will take the visual schedule to the next activity, with* **fewer than 3** *occurrences of screaming or biting his wrist, over three different conditions and maintain for 2 weeks.*

Student's progress toward goal measured by: ☐ Curriculum-based Measures ☒ Behavior Observation ☐ Skills Checklist ☐ Work Sample ☐ Test Results ☐ Other _____

6. **FUNCTIONAL LIFE SKILLS:** *When Tabib is ready to go outside, he will correctly put on and fasten his coat within 3 minutes with no prompts, 4/5 times weekly with 2 different coats, for 4 consecutive weeks.*

Benchmarks/Short-term Objectives

a. *When directed by the teacher, Tabib will correctly* **get his coat** *within 1 minute, 4/5 times without prompting, with 2 different coats.*

b. *After getting his coat, Tabib will correctly* **put it on** *within 2 minutes, 4/5 times without prompting, with 2 different coats.*

c. *After putting on his coat, Tabib will correctly* **fasten it** *within 3 minutes, 4/5 times without prompting, with 2 different coats, and maintain this skill for at least 4 weeks.*

Student's progress toward goal measured by: ☐ Curriculum-based Measures ☐ Behavior Observation ☒ Skills Checklist ☐ Work Sample ☐ Test Results ☐ Other _____

Services to Achieve Annual Goals and Advance in General Curriculum

Special Education Services   R = *Regular class*   S = *Special class*   O = *Other*   D = *Daily*   W = *Weekly*   M = *Monthly*

Service	Location	Time	Frequency	Begin date	Duration
Specially designed instruction	R (S) O:	*3 hrs.*	(D) W M	*9/16*	(1 yr) O:
Specially designed instruction	(R) S O:	*3 hrs.*	(D) W M	*9/16*	(1 yr) O:

Related Services to Benefit from Special Education

Service	Location	Time	Frequency	Begin date	Duration
Speech-language services	R (S) O:	*45 min.*	(D) W M	*9/16*	(1 yr) O:

Program Modifications and/or Supplementary Aids and Services in Regular Classes

Modifications/Personnel Support	Frequency	Supplementary Aids and Services	Frequency
Autism training and consultation	D W (M)	*Personal communication device*	(D) W M

Applicable Special Factors

Factor	Not Needed	In IEP
Positive behavior instruction and support when behavior impedes learning of student or others		✔
Language needs for student with limited English proficiency	✔	
Braille instruction for student who is blind or visually impaired	✔	
Communication and/or language services for student who is deaf, hard of hearing, or has other communication needs		✔
Assistive technology devices or services		✔

Participation in Regular Class, Extracurricular and Nonacademic Activities

The student will participate in the regular class, extracurricular and nonacademic activities except as noted above and listed here: ☒ *Tabib will not participate in lunch in the cafeteria at the same time as other students or in school assemblies.*

Schedule for Written IEP Progress Reports to Parents

☒ Weekly   ☐ Bi-weekly   *via*   ☒ Progress report   ☒ Report card
☐ Monthly   ☐ Quarterly   ☒ Home note   ☒ Parent Conference

Transition Plan

Complete and attach for students age 16 and older.

Participation in State and District Assessments

Participation Codes

S	Standard administration	No accommodations or modifications
A	Participate with accommodations	Does not invalidate, alter, or lower standard
M	Participate with modifications	Invalidates, alters, or lowers standard
AA	Participate using alternate assessment: ☐ Out-of-level CRT ☒ State alternate assessment	Aligned more closely with alternate curriculum than general education curriculum

State and District Assessment Matrix

Enter appropriate participation code for each applicable assessment.

Grade	Kindergarten Pretest	Kindergarten Posttest	State Criterion Referenced Math	State Criterion Referenced Language Arts	State Criterion Referenced Science	Iowa Test of Basic Skills	National Assessment Educational Progress
K							
1			AA	AA	AA	AA	AA
2							
3							
4							
5							
6							
7							
8							
9							
10							
11							
12							

Accommodations and Modifications

List specific accommodations and modifications for assessments.

N/A

Alternate Assessment

State why student cannot participate in regular assessment: *Tabib requires substantial modifications to meaningfully access the grade-level content and requires intensive individualized instruction in order to acquire and generalize knowledge.*

State why selected alternate assessment is appropriate: *The selected alternate assessment aligns with the substantial modifications and intensive individualized instruction necessary for Tabib to acquire and generalize grade-level knowledge.*

Student *Tabib Wilson*   Date ___*Sept. 15*___

IEP Team Participants

Whitney & Larry Wilson   Parent

Janelle Saunders   LEA Representative

_____   Student

Georgia McCandless   Regular Class Teacher

Eula Burton   Special Education Teacher

AARON ALLEN-HATCH   School Psychologist

Kathy Bova   Speech-Language Pathologist

_____   _____

If parent signature missing, provide copy of IEP and Procedural Safeguards and check below:

☐ Did not attend (document efforts to involve parent)

☐ Via telephone

☐ Other _____

Comments

ISABEL ROJAS

Isabel Rojas is a 20-year-old Hispanic young woman who is diagnosed with Down syndrome and educationally classified as having mental retardation.

Family and Cultural Background

Isabel lives at home with her mother. Isabel has an older brother and a younger sister who are attending the state university and an older sister who is married and has two children. Mr. Rojas passed away during Isabel's junior year in high school; Isabel she still cries herself to sleep at night, sobbing that she misses her papa. Mrs. Rojas works full-time as a housekeeper at an upscale hotel and has limited proficiency in English. Mr. and Mrs. Rojas emigrated from Mexico shortly after learning Isabel had Down syndrome. Mrs. Rojas has been very appreciative of the education provided to Isabel, and has respected school personnel by accepting all of their educational recommendations. However, she has told her other children that she hopes for the day when Isabel can work for the local International Food Store, owned and operated by Mrs. Rojas' brother, Giovanni Ruiz. She feels confident that this would provide life-long employment for Isabel, whereas she is not as trusting of a commercial chain store to care as much about the special needs and circumstances of her daughter.

Prior School Experience

Isabel was diagnosed as having Down syndrome shortly after her birth. She received early intervention services in the home and at the Early Education Center, attended a preschool for students with developmental delays, and progressed through elementary and secondary school in classes for students with disabilities and in classes alongside her nondisabled peers. In her senior year of high school, she was elected Homecoming Queen, and has since named herself "Queen Isabel."

Current Schooling

After completion of her senior year, Isabel enrolled in the school district post-secondary vocational program for students with disabilities: the Life and Learning Program. This program is housed at the local community college, and is attended by 85 students aged 18–21. Of these students, 59% (50) are white; 21% (18) are Hispanic; 5% (4) are Asian; and 15% (13) are from other ethnic/racial categories. Also, 31% (26) have limited English proficiency.

At the community college she is enrolled in a Pilates class, a drama class, and sings with the campus choir. She also is enrolled in daily life skills and employability classes through the special education program. She works three hours a day as a greeter at Wal-Mart and is paid a competitive wage. She is supported by a job coach for one hour each day. Isabel enjoys her work and wants to continue her employment at Wal-Mart.

Isabel's teacher, Mr. Polaski, coordinates the educational classes and career training for 15 students who have intellectual disabilities needing limited or intermittent support. The curriculum is individualized for the students according to their Individualized Education Programs. The students have opportunities to take classes at the college, complete apprenticeships, and hold jobs in the community.

Relevant Instructional and Behavioral Information

Functional Academics. Isabel can compute addition and subtraction problems with four digits using a calculator, but computes 2-digit multiplication and division problems with 50% accuracy. When asked, Isabel can give the names and values of coins, can count coins to values to $1, and can use the "dollar more" strategy to values of $20. She does not correctly write checks when purchasing items. She can read a digital clock to the minute, but only to the hour on an analog clock.

Isabel can read books written in English on a 2.5 grade level, but her comprehension is on a 1st grade level. She enjoys books about young adults, but gets frustrated because of the reading skills necessary for reading such books. Isabel enjoys writing in English about events of the day in her electronic diary (on a handheld computer she uses at school). Her writing composition is on a 2nd grade level; however, she uses a spellchecker with 50% accuracy to check her work (she has difficulty choosing the right spelling for the word she is checking).

Social/Emotional. Isabel is highly social, and loves to tease her friends in a playful way. When required to complete difficult or "boring" tasks, Isabel often avoids these tasks by talking with her friends, and it often takes 5–10 verbal prompts to get Isabel to begin the task. Once she begins, she almost always completes the task. When she is tired she exhibits extreme emotions: uncontrollable giggling, sobbing, and occasional anger, approximately 5 times per week. She learns best when she can have fun or play games, is supported in her personal choices, and is given opportunities for social growth.

Communication. Isabel is able to speak both in English and in Spanish, communicating many of her wants/needs, transferring information, using social etiquette, and engaging in conversation for social closeness. She also engages in self-talk to regulate her emotions; however, she often gets "stuck" talking about negative feelings such as anger, frustration, sorrow, and jealousy, and is unable to resolve these issues by herself. Isabel's intelligibility is not clear, especially for those not familiar with her, and she is unable to repair conversations when they break down.

Functional Life Skills. Isabel has recently learned to use the city bus system to get to the community college, but is unable to take the bus to other places which are important to her, such as the mall and the movie theater. She can shop at the grocery store with personal support, and can make three simple cold meals using a specialized picture-based cookbook and verbal support from an adult. Isabel's mother was asked to provide recipes for some of the family's favorite simple hot meals. These recipes and accompanying pictures have been added to her recipe book, but Isabel has not yet learned to make hot meals.

Career/Vocational. Isabel participated in a job sampling program when she was in high school and determined that she enjoys being a greeter at Wal-Mart more than other jobs; however, her manager, Shirley McMahon, indicates that she chats too much with the customers. Her manager sees Isabel's potential to expand her skill set and wants her to learn to stock shelves and gather and return shopping carts, along with being a greeter. Isabel has not yet learned to perform these tasks, and she is apprehensive about doing these jobs, for fear that she will lose her job as a greeter.

INDIVIDUALIZED EDUCATION PROGRAM

Student _Isabel Rojas_   Birth date _April 15_   IEP Date _April 20_

School _Life and Learning Center_   Grade _12+_   Classification _Mental Retardation_

Present Levels of Academic Achievement and Functional Performance

Preschool students: Describe how the disability affects the student's participation in appropriate activities.

School-age students: Describe how the disability affects the student's involvement and progress in the general curriculum.

MATH: _According to the State Alternate Portfolio Assessment (given April 1–5), Isabel can compute 4-digit addition and subtraction problems using a calculator. She computes 2-digit multiplication and division problems with 50% accuracy. When asked, Isabel can give the names and values of coins, can count coins to values to $1, and can use the "dollar more" strategy to values of $20. She does not correctly write checks when purchasing items. She can read a digital clock to the minute, but only to the hour on an analog clock. Her current math skills are best demonstrated in functional, rather than grade-equivalent curricula._

LANGUAGE ARTS: _Isabel can read English text on a 2.5 grade level, but her comprehension is on a 1st grade level. She can spell on a 2nd grade level, and uses a word-processing spellchecker with 50% accuracy. Isabel does all of her academic work in English._

SOCIAL/EMOTIONAL: _Isabel is very social and loves to tease her friends in a playful way. When required to complete difficult or "boring" tasks, Isabel often avoids these tasks by talking with her friends, and it often takes 5–10 verbal prompts to get Isabel to begin the task. Once she begins, she almost always completes the tasks. When she is tired she exhibits extreme emotions: uncontrollable giggling, sobbing, and occasional anger, approximately 5 times per week (according to parental and teacher report). This inhibits her progress in the general curriculum, as she needs direct instruction of social skills._

COMMUNICATION: _Isabel is able to speak both in English and in Spanish, communicating many of her wants/needs, transferring information, using social etiquette, and engaging in conversation for social closeness. She also engages in self-talk to regulate her emotions; however, she often gets "stuck" talking about feelings such as anger, frustration, sorrow, and jealousy, and is unable to resolve these issues by herself. Isabel's intelligibility is not clear and she is unable to repair conversations with peers when they break down. Her communication skills prevent her from progressing in the general curriculum due to her need for systematic, intense instruction._

FUNCTIONAL LIFE SKILLS: _Isabel has recently learned to use the city bus system to get to the community college, but is unable to take the bus to other places which are important to her, such as the mall and the movie theater. She can shop at the grocery store with personal support, and can make three simple cold meals using a specialized picture-based cookbook and verbal support from an adult. She has not learned to make simple hot meals. Her functional life skills are best met in natural, community-based environments._

CAREER/VOCATIONAL: _Isabel participated in a job sampling program when she was in high school and determined that she enjoys being a greeter at Wal-Mart more than other jobs; however her manager indicates that she chats too much with the customers. She has not yet learned to stock shelves and gather and return shopping carts, and she is apprehensive about doing these jobs, for fear that she will lose her job as a greeter._

Measurable Annual Goals

1. **MATH:** *When assessed on the State Alternate Portfolio Assessment at the end of the school year, Isabel will increase her math skills to at least 80% accuracy in each of the following skill areas: 2-digit multiplication and division problems using a calculator; count coins to values to $5, write a personal check using standard protocol for making purchases, and read time to the minute on an analog clock.*

Benchmarks/Short-term Objectives

a. *When given a functional math task requiring 2-digit multiplication or 2-digit division, Isabel will use a calculator to find the product/quotient, with at least 80% accuracy, in at least two different environments, and maintain the skill for at least 6 weeks.*

b. *When given a stack of coins adding up to no more than $5, Isabel will count the coins with at least 80% accuracy over 10 consecutive trials, and will maintain this skill for at least 6 weeks in at least two different environments.*

c. *When Isabel is purchasing an item that costs more than $20 or is paying a bill, she will use standard check-writing protocol to write checks with at least 4 of the 6 components completed correctly, and maintain this skill for at least one month.*

d. *When it is time to switch an activity (e.g., catch the bus, clock in at work, go to class) and only analog clocks are available, Isabel will state the time to the minute with at least 80% accuracy over at least 20 trials, and maintain this skill for at least 3 weeks.*

Student's progress toward goal measured by: ☒ Curriculum-based Measures ☐ Behavior Observation ☒ Skills Checklist ☐ Work Sample ☐ Test Results ☐ Other _____

2. **LANGUAGE ARTS:** *When assessed at the end of the school year, Isabel will compose, illustrate, spellcheck, and read her own stories with at least 80% accuracy, with at least 3 different stories to 3 different audiences.*

Benchmarks/Short-term Objectives

a. *When given a picture-based word-processing program, Isabel will write a creative story by selecting pictures and typing in text, with at least 80% of the words spelled correctly, for at least 3 stories on different topics.*

b. *When given a text-based word-processing program, Isabel will write a creative story by typing in text and using the spellchecker to correct spelling errors, with at least 80% of the words spelled correctly, for at least 3 stories on different topics.*

c. *Using a story Isabel has written, she will insert clip art from a software program or from the Internet to illustrate her story, with no more than 10 verbal prompts per story, for at least 3 different stories.*

d. *With the illustrated story Isabel has created, she will read her story to an audience, with no more than 5 reading errors, reading at least 3 different stories to 3 different audiences.*

Student's progress toward goal measured by: ☐ Curriculum-based Measures ☐ Behavior Observation ☒ Skills Checklist ☐ Work Sample ☐ Test Results ☐ Other _____

3. **SOCIAL/EMOTIONAL:** *When required to complete difficult or "boring" tasks, Isabel will complete the task before spending free time with her friends, with fewer than 3 prompts to begin the task. Rather than talking to herself or others about extreme emotions she is experiencing, Isabel will write her feelings in her electronic journal, then discuss possible solutions with a teacher or other adult at least 90% of observed occurrences for at least one month.*

Benchmarks/Short-term Objectives

a. *When required to complete a difficult or "boring" task and given a 5-minute advance-notice, Isabel will begin the task with fewer than 3 prompts to begin the task, over 5 consecutive school days, and with at least 3 different types of tasks.*

b. *When Isabel is feeling extreme emotions, she will use her handheld computer or personal computer to write about these emotions in her electronic diary, with no more than three verbal prompts to write, for at least three different emotions, at least 90% of the time, over a period of at least one month.*

c. *After having written about her emotions in her diary, Isabel will engage in a verbal problem-solving session with a teacher or other adult support personnel until a reasonable solution can be planned, at least 90% of the time, over a period of at least one month.*

Student's progress toward goal measured by: ☐ Curriculum-based Measures ☒ Behavior Observation ☒ Skills Checklist ☐ Work Sample ☐ Test Results ☐ Other _____

4. **COMMUNICATION:** *When engaged in conversation, Isabel will increase her speech intelligibility and repair conversational breakdowns, at least 80% of observed occurrences.*

Benchmarks/Short-term Objectives

a. *When speaking to a new friend or an acquaintance, Isabel will enunciate all of her words so that her main message is intelligible at least 80% of the observed occurrences, and will maintain this skill for at least one month in at least two different settings.*

b. *After a conversation has broken down, Isabel will use repair strategies (e.g., asking for clarification, asking to repeat statements) at least 80% of the observed occurrences, with at least 3 communication partners, and maintain this skill for at least 1 month in at least 2 different settings.*

Student's progress toward goal measured by: ☐ Curriculum-based Measures ☐ Behavior Observation ☒ Skills Checklist ☐ Work Sample ☐ Test Results ☐ Other _____

5. **FUNCTIONAL LIFE SKILLS:** *When given pictorial support, Isabel will use the city bus system, shop at the grocery store, and prepare simple hot and cold meals with at least 80% accuracy and maintain for two months.*

Benchmarks/Short-term Objectives

a. *When scheduled to go to the mall, movie theatre, or the International Food Market and given picture-based cues, Isabel will accurately use the city bus to arrive safely and on time, with 100% accuracy and with no personal assistant, and maintain this skill for at least two months.*

b. *When given a visual support system (written and picture-based cues), Isabel will purchase grocery items needed to make a meal, with at least 80% accuracy, and maintain this skill for at least two months.*

c. *When given a picture-based cookbook, Isabel will select and make at least 7 cold meals and 3 hot meals with no verbal prompting, for at least 8 different meals, and maintain this skill for two months.*

Student's progress toward goal measured by: ☐ Curriculum-based Measures ☐ Behavior Observation ☒ Skills Checklist ☐ Work Sample ☐ Test Results ☐ Other _____

6. **CAREER/VOCATIONAL:** *When working in a store, Isabel will complete assigned tasks with at least 80% accuracy and maintain for at least 4 weeks.*

Benchmarks/Short-term Objectives

a. *When given five sets of items to stock, Isabel will stock the items on the appropriate shelves, with at least 80% accuracy, over 20 trials, maintaining this skill for at least 4 weeks.*

b. *When asked to gather the grocery carts, Isabel will gather all carts found in the cart-return area and return them to their appropriate location, within 10 minutes, and maintain this skill for at least 4 weeks.*

c. *When greeting shoppers at the store, Isabel will greet them with social etiquette statements (e.g., "Hello," "How are you?," "Welcome") and not with social closeness statements (e.g., "Guess what I did last night?" "Do you have a boyfriend?"), at least 90% of observed occurrences, and in at least two settings, and maintain this skill for at least 4 weeks.*

Student's progress toward goal measured by: ☐ Curriculum-based Measures ☒ Behavior Observation ☒ Skills Checklist ☐ Work Sample ☐ Test Results ☐ Other

Services to Achieve Annual Goals and Advance in General Curriculum

Special Education Services   R = *Regular class* S = *Special class* O = *Other* D = *Daily* W = *Weekly* M = *Monthly*

Service	Location	Time	Frequency	Begin date	Duration
Specially designed instruction	R ⓈO:	*5 hrs.*	D ⓌM	*4/21*	①yr O:
Specially designed instruction	ⓇS O:	*10 hrs.*	D ⓌM	*4/21*	①yr O:
Specially designed instruction	R S Ⓞ *Store*	*15 hrs.*	D ⓌM	*4/21*	①yr O:

Related Services to Benefit from Special Education

Service	Location	Time	Frequency	Begin date	Duration
Speech-language services	R ⓈO:	*60 min.*	D ⓌM	*4/21*	①yr O:

Program Modifications and/or Supplementary Aids and Services in Regular Classes

Modifications/Personnel Support	Frequency	Supplementary Aids and Services	Frequency
Training for store manager	D W Ⓜ	*Handheld computer*	Ⓓ W M

Applicable Special Factors

Factor	Not Needed	In IEP
Positive behavior instruction and support when behavior impedes learning of student or others		✔
Language needs for student with limited English proficiency		✔
Braille instruction for student who is blind or visually impaired	✔	
Communication and/or language services for student who is deaf, hard of hearing, or has other communication needs		✔
Assistive technology devices or services		✔

Participation in Regular Class, Extracurricular and Nonacademic Activities

The student will participate in the regular class, extracurricular and nonacademic activities except as noted above and listed here: ☒ *Isabel will participate in elective classes with her nondisabled peers at the community college, except for when she is in her life skills and employability classes, and when she is working.*

Schedule for Written IEP Progress Reports to Parents

☐ Weekly   ☒ Bi-weekly ⎤ *via* ⎡ ☒ Progress report   ☐ Report card

☐ Monthly   ☐ Quarterly ⎦   ⎣ ☒ Home note   ☐ Parent Conference

Transition Plan

Complete and attach for students age 16 and older. *See Attached.*

Participation in State and District Assessments

Participation Codes

S	Standard administration	No accommodations or modifications
A	Participate with accommodations	Does not invalidate, alter, or lower standard
M	Participate with modifications	Invalidates, alters, or lowers standard
AA	Participate using alternate assessment: ☐ Out-of-level CRT ☐ State alternate assessment	Aligned more closely with alternate curriculum than general education curriculum

State and District Assessment Matrix   Enter appropriate participation code for each applicable assessment.

Grade	Kindergarten Pretest	Kindergarten Posttest	State Criterion Referenced Math	State Criterion Referenced Language Arts	State Criterion Referenced Science	Iowa Test of Basic Skills	National Assessment Educational Progress
K							
1							
2							
3							
4							
5							
6							
7							
8							
9							
10							
11							
12							

Accommodations and Modifications   List specific accommodations and modifications for assessments.

N/A

Alternate Assessment

State why student cannot participate in regular assessment: *Regular assessment is not required for Isabel's nondisabled peers (age 20); therefore, there is no state or district-wide assessment in which she would participate.*

State why selected alternate assessment is appropriate: *Curriculum-based and community-based alternate assessment will occur in order to provide appropriate instructional goals for Isabel.*

Student *Isabel Rojas*   Date *April 20*

IEP Team Participants

Signature	Role
Carmen Rojas	Parent
STEVEN JORGENSEN	LEA Representative
Isabel Rojas	Student
Chloe Daniels	Regular Class Teacher
Tom Dolaski	Special Education Teacher
Manuel Guzman	School Psychologist
Miriam Sanchez	Speech-Language Pathologist
SHIRLEY MCMAHON	Wal-Mart Manager
Giovanni Ruiz	International Food Market
Leilani Hamamoto	Vocational Rehabilitation

If parent signature missing, provide copy of IEP and Procedural Safeguards and check below:

☐ Did not attend (document efforts to involve parent)

☐ Via telephone

☐ Other _____

Comments

TRANSITION PLAN

Student _Isabel Rojas_   Birth date _April 15_ Age _20_ IEP Date _April 20_

Transition Goals, Activities, and Services

Write the transition activities and services needed to achieve postsecondary goals. Refer to IEP goals or explain how transition activities/services will be provided. Indicate who is responsible and why services may not be needed.

1. **Functional Vocational Evaluation.**

Services needed to achieve goals	Agency responsible
Administer functional vocational evaluation	_Vocational Rehabilitation_

   OR indicate why service is not needed:

   ☐ Student functions independently in work settings.

   ☒ Other: _While Isabel works with minimal supervision from a job coach at Wal-Mart, Mrs. Rojas would like Isabel to begin working at the International Food Market. An evaluation of the demands of this job and Isabel's skills will need to be conducted._

2. **Education.** See IEP goal(s) # _1–4_ , or indicate here:

   ☐ Graduate with a regular diploma   ☒ Post-secondary education

   ☒ Graduate with a certificate of completion   ☐ Other: _____

Services needed to achieve goals	Agency responsible
Life and Learning Program	_School district_
Community College classes	_School district_

3. **Training.** See IEP goal(s) # _6_ , or list here:

Skill training goals:
Job training goals:

Services needed to achieve goals	Agency responsible
Job Coach	_School district_

   OR indicate why service is not needed:

   ☐ Student functions independently in work settings.

   ☐ Other: _____

4. **Employment.** See IEP goal(s) # _6_ , or list here:

Services needed to achieve goals	Agency responsible
On-the-job training	_Wal-Mart;_
	International Food Market

   OR indicate why service is not needed:

   ☐ Student functions independently in work settings.

   ☐ Other: _____

5. Independent Living. See IEP goal(s) # _____5_____ , or indicate here:

Housing

- ☐ Skilled Care Facility
- ☐ Group Home
- ☐ Supervised Apartment
- ☐ Supported Living
- ☒ Family home
- ☐ Apartment
- ☐ Home of own
- ☐ Other: _____

Transportation

- ☐ Independent transportation (e.g., walk, bicycle, car)
- ☒ Public transportation (e.g., bus, train)
- ☐ Specialized transportation
- ☐ Other: _____

Services needed to achieve goals	Agency responsible
Bus pass	*School district*

OR indicate why service is not needed:

- ☐ Student functions independently.
- ☐ Other: _____

6. Daily Living Skills, if appropriate. See IEP goal(s) # _____5_____ , or list here:

Services needed to achieve goals	Agency responsible
Special education	*School district*

OR indicate why service is not needed:

- ☐ Student functions independently in work settings.
- ☐ Other: _____

Age of Majority

On or before the student's 17th birthday, inform the student and parent(s) of transfer of rights at age 18.
Date informed: *April 2* _____

Nonparticipation in Transition Planning

If the student did not participate in this plan, indicate the steps taken to ensure the student's preferences were considered: _____

_____

If a representative of an agency responsible for providing an activity did not participate, indicate the steps that will be taken to obtain the participation of the agency: _____

_____

Step **1** *Describe the Student's Present Levels of Academic Achievement and Functional Performance*

IDEA requires that the IEP include a statement of the student's *Present Levels of Academic Achievement and Functional Performance* (PLAAFP). This is a change from the 1997 law that called for *Present Levels of Educational Performance* (PLEP).

Why is PLAAFP the first step in developing a new IEP?

Stating a student's PLAAFP is the first step because a team must know the student's current levels of achievement and performance in order to set reasonable goals to be achieved in a year's time. You need to know where students are before deciding where you want them to go. The more accurately the team can describe current levels, the more likely they are to plan appropriate annual goals. For this reason, using current data to describe the student's PLAAFP is the starting point for developing a quality IEP.

What is a PLAAFP Statement?

A PLAAFP statement is a brief but detailed description of a student's achievement and performance at the time the IEP is written, including all areas affected by the disability.

As you can see, the new term is more descriptive than *present levels of educational performance,* mentioning both academic and functional performance levels rather than just *educational performance.* Let's take a look at these two terms.

- **Academic achievement** refers to gaining requisite skills and knowledge for success in school. The most important academic skills students learn are reading, writing, and math because these skills are foundational for achievement in other academic areas such as science, health, and social studies.

- **Functional performance** can be defined as applying knowledge and skills to meet everyday needs. These functional skills can include activities such as feeding and dressing oneself, participating in recreational activities, engaging in healthy relationships, shopping for groceries, applying and interviewing for a job, and maintaining a bank account.

Why differentiate between academic achievement and functional performance?

Academic achievement and functional performance are differentiated for students depending on their age and on the effects of disability on their learning. Most students' education will focus primarily on the general curriculum, so their PLAAFP statements will center on academic achievement. Other students will need to gain functional living skills; therefore, their PLAAFP statements will describe functional performance. Some students may require statements in both areas.

Generally, the larger the gap between a student's academic or functional performance and age-appropriate core curriculum, the more likely the student's IEP will address functional living skills. For example, a five-year-old child who does not correctly identify colors may have an academic goal for obtaining this skill. However, an eighteen-year-old student who does not correctly identify colors might have a more functional goal to prepare for adult living, such as sorting dark and light colors for laundry.

Why are PLAAFP statements important?

PLAAFP statements provide a starting point for all decisions regarding a student's individualized education. Teachers must understand what students know before teaching them something new. What if a teacher were to ask a student to read *The Cat in the Hat* by Dr. Seuss when the student had never learned letter names or sounds? The result? Failure and frustration, because there is a significant mismatch between what the student can do and what the teacher is asking. Knowing the student's reading skill level will guide the teacher toward an appropriate starting point. Likewise, accurate PLAAFP statements guide IEP teams toward appropriate goals for improvement.

Where do I get information to develop PLAAFP statements?

Information to develop PLAAFP statements is obtained from assessment data, by observation, and from parents or other caregivers who know the student well. To develop a relevant PLAAFP statement you should do the following:

- **Determine the student's current *academic* strengths and needs.**

    Each student's academic strengths and needs are identified by formal and informal assessment. Intelligence tests broadly measure aptitude for learning, indicating a student's ability to process information as required for learning. Common standardized IQ tests include the *Wechsler Intelligence Scale for Children* and the *Stanford-Binet Intelligence Scales.*

    Achievement in specific academic areas can be assessed with standardized, norm-referenced tests, which compare students' achievement to that of national populations. These include tests such as the *Woodcock-Johnson Psychoeducational Battery,* the *Wechsler Individual Achievement Test,* and other standardized achievement tests.

    Informal assessment may include using criterion-referenced tests that compare student achievement to set criteria. Such tests include the *Brigance Comprehensive Inventory of Basic Skills, Dynamic Indicators of Basic Early Literacy Skills, Wide-Range Achievement Test,* core curriculum tests designed by state offices of education, and alternate assessments designed for students with significant cognitive disabilities.

    Other informal assessments include curriculum-based tests that measure student performance directly from the current curriculum, such as placement tests for a math program or tests to check vocabulary knowledge prior to teaching a new science unit.

    Parents or other caregivers are valuable sources of information about students. They know the student better than the school does and can give insight into the individual's interests, hobbies, and talents. Parents can also enlighten the team regarding a student's history of success or failure and strategies that have worked well in the past.

Data from these various assessments are then summarized to describe the student's present levels of academic achievement. At this point, the IEP team knows the upper level of the individual's academic skills.

- **Determine the student's current *functional* strengths and needs.**

   Each student's functional strengths and needs are identified by formal and informal assessment. Formal assessments include standardized norm-referenced tests, such as the *Vineland Adaptive Behavior Scales, Scales of Independent Behavior,* and the *American Association on Mental Retardation Adaptive Behavior Scales,* which are often used to compare students' functional skills to those of national populations. Also included are formal assessments, such as the *Behavior Observation Sequence* and the *Behavior Assessment System for Children,* which measure students' prosocial or maladaptive behavior. These assessments are completed by classroom teachers, school psychologists, and parents.

   Informal assessment involves criterion-referenced tests that compare students' functional skills to set criteria. These tests include the *Brigance Diagnostic Inventory of Early Development, Checklist of Adaptive Living Skills,* and alternate assessments designed for students with significant cognitive disabilities.

   Collaboration with parents when assessing functional skills is critical. What is functional at school may not be functional at home, and vice versa, so school professionals and parents must work closely together to describe students' present levels of functional performance across environments.

   Data from various assessments are then summarized to describe students' present levels of functional performance.

- **Determine how the *academic* and *functional* skills and needs of this student differ from appropriate levels of achievement for nondisabled students of the same age.**

   Formal assessment data indicate the student's achievement compared to a broad population in the same age or grade level. Only current data are used to develop PLAAFP statements, as they are often used for discrepancy-based eligibility determination.

   Criterion-referenced test results show the student's achievement relative to expected levels for the particular skill. These data are useful for demonstrating the gap between the student's current achievement and that of the average same-age individual.

   Informal assessment helps teachers monitor progress in the student's daily curriculum. These data are most informative for ongoing decisions about teaching and learning; they can be used as often as needed to develop PLAAFP statements.

What are the elements of a PLAAFP statement?

When you write a PLAAFP statement, you should make sure it includes these four elements:

- A description of how the disability affects the student's academic achievement and functional performance in the relevant skill areas

- A description of how the disability affects the student's involvement and progress in the general education curriculum

- For preschool students, as appropriate, a description of how the disability affects the student's participation in appropriate activities

- Sufficient detail to provide logical cues for writing the accompanying annual goals

What does a PLAAFP statement look like?

Here is the PLAAFP statement for math from Herbie's IEP.

Herbie can count to 50, count objects to 50, recognize and write numerals 0–9, and group objects in sets. He recognizes a line, square, and circle, but not a rectangle or triangle. He cannot add or subtract 2 digit by 1 digit problems without regrouping, and has not attempted multiplication. These difficulties in math inhibit his progress in the general curriculum.

Does Herbie's example include the necessary elements?

Yes it does, but let's take a closer look at Herbie's statement so you can see *how* it includes the necessary elements:

- Describes how the disability affects the student's academic achievement and functional performance in the relevant skill areas.

  —*Herbie can count to 50, count objects to 50, recognize and write numerals 0–9, and group objects in sets. He recognizes a line, square, and circle, but not a rectangle or triangle. He cannot add or subtract 2 digit by 1 digit problems without regrouping, and has not attempted multiplication.*

- States how the disability affects the student's involvement and progress in the general education curriculum.

  —*These difficulties in math inhibit his progress in the general curriculum.*

- For preschool students, as appropriate, states how the disability affects the student's participation in appropriate activities.

  —*This does not apply to Herbie since he is in the 3rd grade.*

- Includes sufficient detail to provide descriptive and logical cues for writing the accompanying annual goals.

  —*According to common scope and sequence, beginning 3rd grade students should be able to rote count and write numerals to 999, recognize and draw all basic geometric shapes, and add and subtract 3-digit numbers with renaming.*

Here's a PLAAFP statement from Brittany's IEP:

Brittany reads and comprehends at the 7.0 grade equivalent level, writes accurate sentences and paragraphs, and her math reasoning skills are at the 7.5 grade equivalent level. When directed by the teacher to work independently, she yells defiantly and refuses to begin work 80% of observed instances across settings. When given a variable-time delayed redirection to begin work, she pushes her desktop materials to the floor and puts her head down, 80% of observed instances. She does not ask the teacher for assistance when she does not understand the assignment. Brittany's behaviors inhibit her functional performance and achievement in the general curriculum.

Does Brittany's example include the necessary elements?

Yes it does, but let's look closely at the statement so you can see *how* it includes the necessary elements:

- Describes how the disability affects the student's academic achievement and functional performance in the relevant skill areas

  —*Assignment completion is important to functional performance in the classroom. Brittany's consistent refusal to work on independent assignments and her refusal to ask for assistance negatively affect her achievement.*

- States how the disability affects the student's involvement and progress in the general education curriculum

  —*Brittany's behaviors inhibit her functional performance and achievement in the general curriculum.*

- For preschool students, as appropriate, states how the disability affects the student's participation in appropriate activities

  —*This does not apply to Brittany since she is in the 8th grade.*

- Includes sufficient detail to provide descriptive and logical cues for writing the accompanying annual goals

  —*Yes. Brittany resists teacher direction to work independently and she does not ask for assistance when needed, so her IEP goals must address starting independent work when directed by the teacher and asking the teacher for assistance when she needs help on an assignment.*

Here are assessment data for Samuel, a 5th grade student with mental retardation. Your task is to summarize the data into a brief but descriptive PLAAFP for Samuel's IEP. When you have finished, check your PLAAFP with our suggestion in the Appendix.

Achievement Testing

Math Calculation: 9/10 one-digit addition and subtraction correct; 0/10 2-digit and 1 digit without renaming correct; 0/5 multiplication and division correct.

Written expression: Dictates simple sentences when given a concrete subject, 5/5 correct; writes simple sentences when given a concrete subject, 0/5 correct.

Functional Skills Assessment

Self-Help Skills: Correctly identifies his backpack, but does not place school materials in the backpack when directed. Uses the restroom independently, but does not zip pants or wash hands afterwards.

Socialization: Follows 2-step requests in order and talks with his friends. He does not wait his turn in line, and he interrupts others in their conversations.

PLAAFP for Samuel:

_____

_____

_____

Oops!

Here are common errors in writing PLAAFP statements:

- Writing a statement with vague descriptions of achievement or performance
  "Rico is earning a C– in math."
  "Randy's reading standard score is 84."
  "LaFawnduh can't control her behaviors in public."

- Writing a statement that is not related to the student's curriculum
  "Vern is very helpful at home."
  "Pedro is doing a good job being his Boy Scout patrol leader."
  "Tina always eats her breakfast."

- Writing a statement that is not related to the student's disability
  "Deb [with a reading disability] has excellent grades in band and chorus."
  "Rex [a 5-year-old who stutters] knows his colors and shapes."
  "Starla [who has cerebral palsy and uses a wheelchair] is earning a B in science."

- Writing a statement with only strengths but no logical cues for writing goals in areas needing improvement

  "Suzanne knows her letter names and sounds and can sound out simple words."

  "Napoleon behaves appropriately in a well-structured setting."

  "Rodrigo has learned to ride the bus independently."

- For a preschooler, writing a statement which does not state how the disability affects the student's participation in appropriate activities

  "Ilene, who is 3 years old, is unable to state her birth date."
  (Most 3-year-olds cannot do this, so it is not an "appropriate activity.")

  "Renae, who is 4 years old, cannot sit for more than 30 minutes to listen to the teacher read a story."
  (4-year-olds are not expected to sit and listen for 30 minutes, so this is not an "appropriate activity.")

  "Don, who is 4 years old, is unable to match lower-case letters on a worksheet."
  (4-year-olds generally do not study the alphabet in such detail, so this is not an "appropriate activity.")

NOW YOU TRY SOME.

For each incomplete or poorly written PLAAFP statement below, indicate the common errors. Check your answers with ours in the Appendix.

1. *"Lance (a 14-year-old boy) initiates and sustains conversations with peers and can call his friends on the telephone."*

   Common Error: _____

2. *"Nathan (a 9-year-old boy with specific learning disabilities in reading) writes all upper- and lower-case letters in isolation and in words. He does not form closed letters correctly. His penmanship skills inhibit his progress in the general writing curriculum."*

   Common Error: _____

3. *"Corina (6-year-old girl) is often out of control and is unhappy with school."*

   Common Error: _____

Let's review the elements of a PLAAFP statement.

A PLAAFP statement should include these four elements:

- A description of how the disability affects the student's academic achievement and functional performance in relevant skill areas

- A statement of how the disability affects the student's involvement and progress in the general education curriculum

- For preschool students, as appropriate, an explanation of how the disability affects the student's participation in appropriate activities

- Sufficient detail to provide descriptive and logical cues for writing the accompanying annual goals

CONGRATULATIONS! YOU HAVE COMPLETED STEP 1. LET'S MOVE ON TO **STEP 2,** WRITING GOALS FOR IMPROVEMENT.

✔ Describe the student's present levels of academic achievement and functional performance.

2 Write measurable annual goals.

3 Measure and report student progress.

4 State the services needed to achieve annual goals.

5 Explain the extent, if any, to which the student will not participate with nondisabled students in the regular class and in extracurricular and other nonacademic activities.

6 Explain accommodations necessary to measure academic achievement and functional performance on state and district-wide assessments.

7 Complete a transition plan for students aged 16 and older.

Step **2** *Write Measurable Annual Goals*

You have learned that statements of present levels of academic achievement and functional performance describe how a student's disability affects involvement and progress in the general education curriculum. In this section you will learn that a list of measurable annual goals designates what the student is expected to achieve in the next year to address the effects of the disability. You might say that *present levels* reflect *present* conditions, and *annual goals* describe expected achievement *within the next year*.

What are measurable annual goals?

Measurable annual goals are the IEP team's best estimate of what the student can accomplish in the next year. A statement of measurable academic and functional performance goals must do the following:

- Meet the student's needs related to the disability that may interfere with his or her involvement and progress in the general education curriculum

- Meet the student's additional educational needs resulting from the disability

- Be measurable

What is the general education curriculum?

The general curriculum is established by state offices of education and implemented in individual schools under the direction of school districts. Some state curricula consist of a general scope and sequence for each grade level. Other states have developed more specific measurable outcomes for each subject area in each grade. Students with disabilities are expected to receive appropriate instruction in math, reading, writing, social studies, science and other content, as are nondisabled students.

What are "additional educational needs resulting from the disability?"

IDEA requires teams to consider a student's academic, developmental, and functional needs. Since *general education curriculum* refers mainly to academic subjects, *additional educational needs* refers to the student's developmental and functional needs that directly result from the disability. *Developmental* refers to a predictable sequence of growth. Therefore, a student with developmental needs may fall considerably behind peers in such areas as self-care, language, or motor skills. *Functional* refers to applying knowledge and skills to meet everyday needs such as eating, dressing, mobility, communication, and transportation. A preschool child's curriculum may focus on developmental growth, whereas an adolescent's curriculum may focus on functional living skills.

What does *measurable* mean?

Measurable means the behavior stated in the goal can be observed and measured to determine when it has been achieved. For example, *understand addition* is not observable or measurable because it is not clear how the student will demonstrate understanding. You cannot see a student *understand;* you can only see *evidence* of understanding in some observable form. Stated in measurable terms, the goal might be "write correct answers to addition problems." You can observe written answers and easily measure their accuracy.

How does the IEP team set goals that are important to the student and the family?

You'll remember that the IEP team includes relevant school professionals, the parents or guardians, and the student when appropriate. Each team member contributes important perspectives toward setting appropriate goals. Let's look at each member's contributions.

- **Parents.** Parents know much about what the student can reasonably accomplish, based on their child's history in the home and at school. It is essential that the parent perspective is not only considered, but included in goal setting. Too often parents are marginalized in the goal-setting process by school personnel who are more concerned with having the student fit in with existing classroom curriculum and routines.

- **Regular classroom teacher.** The regular classroom teacher understands the general curriculum and can guide the team to align IEP goals with it.

- **Special education teacher.** The special education teacher can break down the general curriculum standards or instructional tasks in the areas affected by the student's disability in order to write reasonable goals for achievement within the year.

- **Related services providers.** The related service providers assess the student in areas affected by the disability such as speech and language, fine and gross motor skills, or emotional disturbance. These professionals provide information from their assessments to help the team develop goals for improvement in their areas of specialty.

- **Local education agency (LEA) representative.** The LEA representative verifies the availability of resources necessary to achieve the goals.

- **Individual(s) who can interpret evaluation results.** A teacher or related services provider who can explain test results should be included so that team members can understand and use the results to determine appropriate goals. For example, a special education teacher can interpret achievement test results, a school psychologist can explain psychological test results, and an occupational therapist can explain the results of fine motor skill assessment.

- **Other individuals with special knowledge or expertise.** At the discretion of the parent or the school, participants in goal setting may include a family advocate, a cultural/linguistic interpreter, an after-school care provider, or other individual who has relevant knowledge of the disability or of the child as an individual.

- **Student.** Student participation in goal setting helps the team understand personal likes, dislikes, and goals for the future. This is very important when the IEP team begins to plan for the student's transition to adult life. Students should be invited to take part in the IEP planning when they are able to contribute.

How do I write a measurable annual goal from the PLAAFP statement?

Remember, the PLAAFP statement describes a student's upper level of current achievement and gives logical cues for new learning. Based on these cues, the annual goal describes the progress the student should be able to make during the following year. Let's look at part of the math example from Herbie's IEP:

- **PLAAFP**

  Herbie can count to 50, count objects to 50, recognize and write numerals 0–9, and group objects in sets. He recognizes a line, square, and circle, but not a rectangle or triangle. He cannot add or subtract 2 digit by 1 digit problems without regrouping, and has not attempted multiplication. These difficulties in math inhibit his progress in the general curriculum.

  - **Cue 1.** Herbie cannot count above 50 or write numbers above 9, which are skills mastered by most 1st graders.

    Annual Goal
    When directed by the teacher, Herbie will rote count and write numbers to 120 with no errors, 3/3 trials over 3 consecutive weeks.

  - **Cue 2.** Herbie cannot recognize a rectangle or triangle.

    Annual Goal
    Given a sheet of geometric shapes Herbie will correctly mark a rectangle, triangle, cube, and cylinder, 2/2 consecutive trials over two weeks.

  - **Cue 3.** Herbie cannot add or subtract 2 digit by 1 digit problems without regrouping.

    Annual Goal
    Given 10 addition and 10 subtraction problems, 3 digit by 3 digit with regrouping, Herbie will solve and write 9/10 answers correctly, 2/2 consecutive trials.

What are the elements of a measurable annual goal?

IDEA 2004, like the previous iterations of the law, does not specify the wording for a measurable annual goal. The law specifies only that annual goals must address progress in the general curriculum, address other needs caused by the disability, and be measurable. IEP teams usually use a format established by the school or district. In addition, best practice suggests that a truly measurable goal has at least three elements.

1. **A description of the CONDITIONS under which the behavior will be performed.** Conditions may include instructional cues, materials, instructional personnel, settings, and time of day. The condition for Herbie's fourth annual goal is "when directed by the teacher."

2. **The specific observable BEHAVIOR to be performed.** This should come from the PLAAFP statement. Observable behaviors are those that the teacher can see or hear. For example, the behavior for Herbie's fourth annual goal is to *rote count* and *write* numbers to 120. The teacher can hear Herbie rote count and can see him write numbers. However, the teacher would not be able to observe how Herbie understands, thinks, or feels about counting and writing numbers. *Understands, thinks,* and *feels* are not observable behaviors; therefore, these terms should not be used in writing annual goals.

Similarly, the phrase *be able to* should not be written in the annual goal, for two reasons. First, students may *be able to* engage in certain behaviors but are prevented from doing so by the conditions. Second, the wording is imprecise. The word *will* is more active and direct.

3. **The CRITERIA to indicate the level of performance at which the goal will be achieved.** The criterion for Herbie's first math goal is "with no errors." Criteria must be related to the behavior. There are many ways to set criteria:

   - *Percentage* is appropriate where the number of trials differs from time to time, such as opportunities to engage in peer play.

   - *Number correct* or *number of allowable errors* is used when the number of trials remains constant, such as 20 spelling words each week.

   - *Rate* refers to speed and accuracy, such as number of words read correctly in one minute or number of math facts written correctly in one minute.

   - *Frequency* is a measure of the number of times a behavior occurs in a set time frame, such as the number of verbal outbursts in a school day.

   - *Latency* measures the time lapse between a stimulus and the desired student response. For instance, the criterion may require a student to respond to an adult's greeting within 15 seconds.

   - *Duration* indicates the length of time a behavior continues, like the number of minutes a student screams before stopping.

   It is very important to choose the appropriate criterion measure for the goal. For instance, a teacher once collected frequency data on student screaming which showed that the student screamed twice per day: once from 8:00 a.m. until lunchtime, and once more from lunch until 3:00 p.m. The teacher quickly realized that duration data were more appropriate.

   Some IEP teams may decide to add two elements to the annual goal:

4. **A statement of GENERALIZATION indicating additional conditions under which the behavior will be performed to criterion.** For Herbie's first goal, generalization could require him to count and write numbers to 120 in a resource classroom and in his regular classroom. Generalization criteria insure that the student can perform the task under various circumstances such as

   - with different people,
   - in various environments,
   - with varied instructional cues.
   - across times of day,
   - with different materials.

5. **A statement of MAINTENANCE for the student to perform the task to criterion for a specified period of time.** The maintenance statement for Herbie requires him to count and write numbers to 120 with no errors 3/3 trials for three consecutive weeks, which shows that he has not only mastered, but also retained the skill.

Why does best practice include these elements for annual goals?

These elements insure that all team members understand and agree on the specific learning or behaviors expected of a student. This is essential for three reasons:

1. Teachers use well-written goals to plan accurate instruction and learning activities for students. Nebulous or nonspecific annual goals are too likely to lead to undirected instruction and wasted learning time.

2. Teachers use the elements to design and administer accurate assessments of student progress toward the annual goals. Continual monitoring guides teachers to make changes in curriculum and instruction if students are not progressing.

3. Team members refer to the elements of well written annual goals to verify the student's final achievement.

May I see nonexamples of measurable annual goals?

Here are two examples that omit important elements.

Example 1: *Edgar will understand how to write accurately.*

YES (NO) Statement of conditions in which behavior will be performed

YES (NO) Statement of observable, measurable behavior

YES (NO) Statement of criterion for mastery

YES (NO) Statement of generalization

YES (NO) Statement of maintenance

Example 2: *When asked by the teacher, Katya will behave appropriately for 3 consecutive weeks.*

(YES) NO Statement of conditions in which behavior will be performed

YES (NO) Statement of observable, measurable behavior

YES (NO) Statement of criterion for mastery

YES (NO) Statement of generalization

(YES) NO Statement of maintenance

NOW IT'S YOUR TURN.

1. Here is an annual goal for Jessica. Write the phrase from the goal next to the matching element in the list below. Then check your answer with our suggestion in the Appendix.

   Annual Goal
   When given a grocery list with 5 or fewer items and a $10.00 bill, Jessica will select and purchase all the items on the list with fewer than 5 prompts in 3 different grocery stores over a three-week period.

   Conditions _____

   Behavior _____

   Criteria _____

   Generalization _____

   Maintenance _____

2. Here is one part of a PLAAPF statement for Morris, a 2nd-grade boy. Your task is to write an annual goal to address this need, making sure to include all five elements. Check your answer with the Appendix.

   PLAAPF Statement
   When directed by the teacher to be seated, Morris yells defiantly and refuses to sit at his desk, 80% of observed instances across settings.

   Conditions _____

   Behavior _____

   Criteria _____

   Generalization _____

   Maintenance _____

Each team might create annual goals that differ from the goals written by other teams, based upon the team's knowledge of the student's preferences and capabilities and the demands of the educational environments in which the student is served. So the goal we suggest in the Appendix will serve only as an example of what a team might decide is appropriate for Morris.

WHAT ABOUT **BENCHMARKS** OR **SHORT-TERM OBJECTIVES** FOR THE ANNUAL GOALS?

Does the IEP team need to include benchmarks or short-term objectives for annual goals?

It depends. Whereas the 1997 reauthorization of IDEA required that all annual goals include benchmarks or short-term objectives, IDEA now requires these provisions only for students who take alternate assessments aligned to alternate achievement standards.

What does this mean for the team?

This means that the IEP team must determine a student's need for alternate assessments aligned to alternate achievement standards and then add benchmarks or short-term objectives to the annual goals. Alternate standards/assessments procedures apply only to the small percentage of students whose disabilities inhibit them from progressing comparably to their peers without disabilities in the general curriculum, and thus they cannot be judged by the same standards. You will learn more about alternate assessments and alternate achievement standards in Step 6.

What are benchmarks and short-term objectives?

Benchmarks and short-term objectives are two ways to break down annual goals into smaller measurable parts. They allow teachers to monitor student achievement in intervals and report progress to IEP team members more than once per year.

- **Benchmarks** describe major milestones anticipated at designated time intervals as the student progresses toward achieving the annual goal.

- **Short-term objectives** break skills into sequential steps that lead to the annual goal.

			Short-term objective	**Annual Goal**
		Short-term objective		
	Short-term objective			
PLAAFP				

Would you explain the terms and accompanying processes in more detail?

Surely. We explain them below.

- **Benchmarks**

   Benchmarks are achievement milestones matched to time intervals: for example, "in 20 weeks," or "by January 30." Annual goals can be broken down into benchmarks in a variety of ways, including accuracy, assistance level, task analysis, and generalization. Here are some sample phrases from benchmarks showing these four ways to break down annual goals:

Accuracy. The goal can be benchmarked according to the level of accuracy required to ensure that the student has acquired the skill or knowledge. For example, benchmarks for accuracy might progress from less accurate to more accurate, as in this example:

- 50% correct by October 31
- 75% correct by January 31
- 90% correct by April 30

Assistance level. The goal can be benchmarked according to the level of assistance needed to complete the task accurately. An example of this progressive assistance level follows:

- With full physical prompting in 10 weeks
- With only verbal prompting in 15 weeks
- With no prompting in 20 weeks

Task analysis. The goal can be task analyzed, or broken down into components to be mastered sequentially in order to accomplish the complete goal. For example, counting to 100 could use these benchmarks:

- Rote count 1–10 in 5 weeks
- Rote count 1–20 (requires teen numbers) in 8 weeks
- Rote count 1–100 (uses the same pattern after 20) in 15 weeks

Generalization. A goal can be benchmarked by increasing levels of generalization to other settings or environments. For example, a goal for the student to totally care for toileting needs may use these benchmarks:

- Totally care for toileting needs in a classroom restroom by November 1
- Totally care for toileting needs in any school restroom by February 1
- Totally care for toileting needs using restrooms in the community by April 1

These criteria are not mutually exclusive. You may decide to combine one or more of them in writing benchmarks for annual goals.

How many benchmarks must the team write?

The law uses the plural terminology "a description of benchmarks or short-term objectives"; thus there must be at least two benchmarks for each annual goal.

May I see an example of a goal with benchmarks?

Here is an example of benchmarks for Tabib using level of assistance:

Annual goal
When children are playing, Tabib will point to the toy he wants to play with and sign (or activate his communication device) "play," without taking the toy from the child, at least 80% of the time with at least 3 different toys and in 3 different settings (free time, recess, structured play time), and maintain for 3 weeks.

Benchmarks

a. In 10 weeks, when children are playing, Tabib will point to the toy he wants to play with and sign or point to "play" with a **full physical prompt** without taking the toy from the child, at least 80% of the time, with at least 3 different toys and in 3 different settings (free time, recess, structured play time), and maintain for 3 weeks.

b. In 20 weeks, when children are playing, Tabib will point to the toy he wants to play with and sign or point to "play" with a **partial physical prompt** without taking the toy from the child, at least 80% of the time, with at least 3 different toys and in 3 different settings (free time, recess, structured play time), and maintain for 3 weeks.

c. In 30 weeks, when children are playing, Tabib will point to the toy he wants to play with and sign or point to "play" with a **teacher model** without taking the toy from the child, at least 80% of the time, with at least 3 different toys and in 3 different settings (free time, recess, structured play time), and maintain for 3 weeks.

Tabib's benchmarks can be illustrated like this:

| PLAAFP | — | Full Prompt | — | Partial prompt | — | Teacher model | — | Sign or point to "play" |

May I see some examples of incompletely written benchmarks?

Here are two examples:

1. *Cleophus will cook a frozen meal in a microwave oven without burning it.*

YES (NO) Statement of conditions in which behavior will be performed

(YES) NO Statement of observable, measurable behavior

(YES) NO Statement of criterion for mastery ("without burning it")

YES (NO) Statement of generalization

YES (NO) Statement of maintenance

YES (NO) Statement of time interval

2. *When Veronica's nose is runny and her teacher asks her to wipe it, she will wipe her nose.*

(YES) NO Statement of conditions in which behavior will be performed

(YES) NO Statement of observable, measurable behavior

YES (NO) Statement of criterion for mastery

YES (NO) Statement of generalization

YES (NO) Statement of maintenance

YES (NO) Statement of time interval

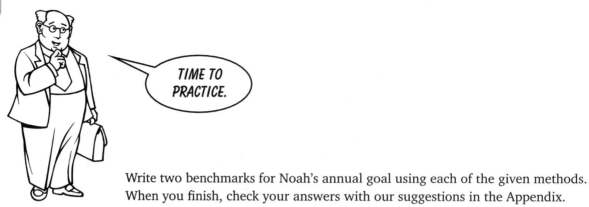

Write two benchmarks for Noah's annual goal using each of the given methods. When you finish, check your answers with our suggestions in the Appendix.

Annual Goal
When presented with 10 items and asked to count them, Noah will point to and orally count the items correctly with no prompts.

Level of Assistance

1. Benchmark: _____

_____

_____

2. Benchmark: _____

_____

_____

Task Analysis

1. Benchmark: _____

_____

_____

2. Benchmark: _____

_____

_____

Generalization

1. Benchmark: _____

_____

_____

2. Benchmark: _____

_____

_____

Short-term Objectives

Short-term objectives break skills into sequential components that lead to the annual goal but are not tied to specific time intervals. Short-term objectives are determined by task analysis. As with benchmarks, task analysis means that the final task is analyzed to determine the sequential subskills that must be mastered to accomplish the goal. Also like benchmarks, short-term objectives describe the conditions, the behavior, and the criteria for mastery. They may also include statements for generalization and maintenance.

Let's look at an example of a short-term objective for Tabib for self-dressing skills.

Annual Goal
When Tabib is ready to go outside, he will correctly put on and fasten his coat within 3 minutes with no prompts, 4/5 times weekly with 2 different coats, for 4 consecutive weeks.

Short-term Objectives

a. When directed by the teacher, Tabib will correctly **get his coat** within 1 minute, 4/5 times without prompting, with 2 different coats.

b. After getting his coat, Tabib will correctly **put it on** within 2 minutes, 4/5 times without prompting, with 2 different coats.

c. After putting on his coat, Tabib will correctly **fasten it** within 3 minutes, 4/5 times without prompting, with 2 different coats, and maintain this skill for at least 4 weeks.

Write two short-term objectives for Noah's annual goal using each of the given methods. When you finish, check your answers with our suggestions in the Appendix.

Annual Goal
When presented with 10 items and asked to count them, Noah will point to and orally count the items correctly with no prompts.

1. Short-term objective: _____

_____

2. Short-term objective: _____

_____

Let's summarize the elements of measurable annual goals, benchmarks, and short-term objectives.

1. Measurable annual goals describe the conditions, the behavior, and the criteria for achievement.

2. They may also contain statements of generalization and maintenance.

3. Benchmarks break down annual goals into smaller measurable parts at designated time intervals.

4. Short-term objectives break down annual goals into sequential components without reference to specific time intervals.

> **EXCELLENT!** YOU HAVE PRACTICED THE SECOND STEP FOR QUALITY IEPs, SO IT'S TIME TO LEARN **STEP 3**.

✔ Describe the student's present levels of academic achievement and functional performance.

✔ Write measurable annual goals.

3 Measure and report student progress.

4 State the services needed to achieve annual goals.

5 Explain the extent, if any, to which the student will not participate with nondisabled students in the regular class and in extracurricular and other nonacademic activities.

6 Explain accommodations necessary to measure academic achievement and functional performance on state and district-wide assessments.

7 Complete a transition plan for students aged 16 and older.

Step

3

Measure and Report Student Progress

We have discussed how important it is to write appropriate annual goals in measurable terms so that the team agrees on the specific expectations for student improvement during the year. Why is measurement so important? Consider this parallel: If you make a New Year's resolution to lose 25 pounds by December but do not weigh yourself until October, you may not meet your goal. Regular weight monitoring would tell you whether or not you are making progress, or if you needed to adjust your behavior. Likewise, when learning is regularly measured, team members know whether or not the student is making adequate progress. If progress is not measured, the team cannot track the success of instruction, and the teacher cannot make necessary changes to help the student meet annual goals.

Parents are part of the team, but they are not in school to observe their children's daily school progress. Therefore, the law requires the team to describe how the school will monitor achievement and to regularly inform parents of student progress toward annual goals. To that end, the IEP must do the following:

- Describe how the student's progress toward meeting the annual goals will be measured

- Describe when periodic reports of the progress the student is making toward meeting the annual goals will be provided

Let's examine each of these in turn.

How do I decide and then describe how the student's progress toward goals will be measured?

You should recall that well written annual goals address progress in the general curriculum and include criteria for achievement. In addition, the IEP must describe **how** those criteria will be measured. It is *essential* that the measurement format

- accurately measures the stated criteria, and

- provides clear evidence of progress in the general curriculum.

The following common methods are often listed on the IEP for measuring progress and achievement:

- **Test results.** Formal tests should accurately align with the desired outcome, whether commercially published, teacher made, or developed at the school, state, or district level.

- **Curriculum-based measurement.** Tests based directly from the student's curriculum are given at more frequent intervals than formal tests.

- **Work samples.** Samples of student work are used to document progress toward the goal.

- **Portfolios.** Collections of student work samples can be used to document progress over time in one or more areas.

- **Teacher observation checklists.** Teachers mark observed progress on charts that they usually make themselves to specifically target individual goals, also called *skills checklists.*

- **Behavior observations.** An observer watches a student and marks a checklist of specific behaviors. Behavior observations are used for tracking appropriate and inappropriate social behaviors rather than academic achievement; they can be completed by any qualified adult observer.

Let's see how this applies to annual goals or benchmarks for Herbie, Tabib, and Brittany.

Herbie's Annual Goal

When directed by the teacher, Herbie will rote count and write numerals to 120 with no errors, on 3/3 trials over 3 consecutive weeks.

Measurement methods
The criteria for achievement are to rote count to 120 and to write the numbers. Appropriate ways to measure these criteria are described here:

- Rote counting can be measured by the teacher observing the skill and recording the data on a **skills checklist.**
  While Herbie counts aloud, the teacher simply records whether or not he counts to 120 correctly for 3 consecutive trials.

- Writing numerals to 120 can be verified by a **curriculum-based measure** in which the teacher directs Herbie to write from 1 to 120.

The two distinct academic tasks in this goal are measured differently, but the criteria for both must be met in order for the goal to be achieved.

Rationale
We chose these methods because rote counting is more readily measured by listening to the student count than by formal tests, portfolios, or behavior observations. Rote counting is a form of curriculum-based measurement, but since it is done orally, the checklist is the hard evidence of achievement. Writing the numbers is a curriculum-based measure that yields its own observable evidence, so this method is selected rather than administering a formal test or using a portfolio or a checklist.

Tabib's Benchmark

When children are playing, Tabib will point to the toy he wants to play with and sign (or activate his communication device) "play" with a teacher model without taking the toy from the child, at least 80% of the time, with at least 3 different toys and in 3 different settings (free time, recess, structured play time), and maintain for 3 weeks.

Measurement method
Signing or pointing to a picture of "play" can be measured by a **behavior observation** or a **skills checklist.** The data must include the number of times weekly and the number of consecutive weeks that the child performs the skill in three different settings.

Rationale

These methods can be used because Tabib's goal includes social and communicative behavior and must be observed in order for achievement to be verified. A checklist on which the teacher can record the results of each trial provides a cumulative record to trace progress and to verify accomplishment of the final goal. Other measurement methods would not be useful in this case.

Brittany's Annual Goal

When directed by the teacher to work independently, Brittany will quietly begin the assignment within 10 seconds, 90% of instances in each of her classes over a 3-week period.

Measurement method

To verify the percentage of instances during which Brittany began her assignments within 10 seconds over the required time period requires a series of **behavior observations.**

Rationale

We chose this method because observations most readily measure progress toward the goal of a specific social behavior. Most behavior changes cannot be measured by formal tests, informal tests, or work samples.

> YOUR TURN!

Read each of the following goals and write two things:

1. An appropriate measurement method
2. Your reason for choosing the method

Jamal's Annual Goal

When presented with 20 items of clothing, Jamal will correctly sort the clothing in preparation for laundering, once weekly for 3 consecutive weeks.

Measurement method _____

Rationale (Why this method?) _____

_____

Bentley's Annual Goal

When given a worksheet with 15 items of each type, Bentley will add and subtract single-digit items and write answers with no errors.

Measurement method _____

Rationale (Why this method?) _____

_____

How do I decide and indicate when periodic reports of progress toward annual goals will be provided?

You must provide regular reports to parents regarding their children's progress, thus updating parents more often than their attendance at annual IEP meetings. The law recommends that reports be issued quarterly or at other regular intervals, such as the times that report cards are sent home. Schools and districts use a variety of reporting methods, and you should check with your supervisors to determine the preferred method in your school.

An IEP form may include a section for indicating when the reporting will be accomplished, such as the one shown here:

Schedule for Written IEP Progress Reports to Parents				
☐ Weekly ☐ Bi-weekly	*via*	☐ Progress report	☒ Report card	
☐ Monthly ☒ Quarterly		☐ Home note	☐ Parent Conference	

How does this step in the IEP process impact classroom practice?

Assessing and reporting each student's progress impacts classroom practice by requiring the teacher to do three things: measure, monitor, and report. *Measuring* is the act of administering some type of assessment to describe student academic or social behavior. *Monitoring* is the act of comparing student achievement to desired goals. *Reporting* provides oral or written information regarding student achievement.

Measuring
A teacher measures progress frequently in order to determine if the students are progressing at the rate necessary to achieve their goals. Informal measures are used more frequently than formal measures, and the measurement schedule depends on the type of learning or behavior to be assessed. The teacher may measure student progress several times a day, once a day, several times a week, once a week, or at some other appropriate interval.

Monitoring
A teacher monitors student progress by comparing measurement data with benchmarks. School-wide student progress is usually compared to state or district standards, grade-level or class progress is often monitored by comparison to other students, and individual progress is compared to individual goals. The latter is the case for students with IEPs. To determine if students are making adequate progress toward IEP goals, a teacher must monitor frequently enough to either verify adequate progress or make necessary instructional changes to increase achievement.

Reporting
Teachers or related service providers use data from teacher monitoring to report students' progress to parents at least as often as described on the IEP.

Let's summarize how to measure and report student progress toward annual goals.

The IEP must do the following:

1. Describe how the student's progress toward meeting the annual goals will be measured.

2. Describe when periodic reports of the progress the student is making toward meeting the annual goals will be provided.

WELL DONE!
YOU HAVE STUDIED AND
PRACTICED STEP 3.
NOW WE WILL MOVE
TO **STEP 4.**

✔ Describe the student's present levels of academic achievement and functional performance.

✔ Write measurable annual goals.

✔ Measure and report student progress.

4 State the services needed to achieve annual goals.

5 Explain the extent, if any, to which the student will not participate with nondisabled students in the regular class and in extracurricular and other nonacademic activities.

6 Explain accommodations necessary to measure academic achievement and functional performance on state and district-wide assessments.

7 Complete a transition plan for students aged 16 and older.

Step **4** *State the Services Needed to Achieve Annual Goals*

The statement of special education and related services on the IEP describes how and where special education will be provided to help students achieve their annual goals. You remember that PLAAFP statements describe what the student is achieving at the time of the IEP and the annual goals describe what the student should achieve in one year. You can think of special education and related services as the bridge between current achievement and achievement in a year's time.

Special education and related services

Current Achievement (PLAAFP)	Achievement in a Year (Annual Goals)

The IEP team reviews the student's current achievement as noted in the PLAAFP statements and they also review the students' annual goals in order to determine which services will be required to meet the annual goals. This review is an important evaluative process wherein team members make collaborative decisions for the student's education based upon empirical evidence. Once services have been determined, then the team determines where these services will be provided.

Unfortunately, some teams make these decisions in a backward fashion. They decide where the student should be served, what services will be provided, then they write the annual goals and PLAAFP statements. Legally correct and quality IEPs are developed with the student's goals driving services and placement.

Special education and related services accomplish two purposes: they help the student achieve annual goals, and they do so in the *least restrictive environment*. Our discussion of special education and related services requires you to understand the least restrictive environment, so we will define this term now.

What is the Least Restrictive Environment?

IDEA requires that students with disabilities be educated in the Least Restrictive Environment (LRE), which means educated with students without disabilities to the maximum extent appropriate, as determined by the IEP team. *Restrictive* in this case means any situation where students with disabilities are educated in special classes, separate schools, or are otherwise removed from the regular class. Removing a student from the regular class is appropriate when the IEP team determines that the nature or severity of the student's disability prevents satisfactory learning, even when supplementary aids or services are provided.

What are possible alternative placements for students with disabilities?

If the IEP team determines that a student's needs cannot be met in the regular class then the team looks at the continuum of alternative placements to meet the student's needs. This continuum moves from least to most restrictive and usually includes the following:

- Full inclusion in regular classes
- Less than one-half day in a resource classroom
- More than one-half day in a resource classroom
- Self-contained classroom within the school
- Instruction in a separate school
- Home instruction
- Instruction in a hospital or institution

Are there other considerations when determining appropriate placement?

Yes. IDEA requires IEP teams to ensure that the student's placement is:

- determined at least annually
- based on the student's IEP
- as close as possible to the student's home. This means the student is educated in the school he or she would attend if not disabled, unless the parent agrees otherwise.

In addition, when selecting the LRE, the team must consider any potential harmful effects on the child or on the quality of services needed. The student should not be removed from an age-appropriate regular class solely because of needed modifications in the general education curriculum. This means that when the student's needs can be met in the regular class by modifying the curriculum or providing other supplemental aids or services, then the student should not be removed to a more restrictive environment.

THAT'S **LRE**. NOW LET'S DISCUSS **SERVICES** TO HELP STUDENTS WITH DISABILITIES ACHIEVE THEIR ANNUAL GOALS.

What services are described on the IEP?

The law requires that the IEP state the services to be provided *to the student* or *on behalf of* the student and also state the program modifications or supports provided for *school personnel* to help the student. IDEA requires that services be based on peer-reviewed research to the extent practicable. This means that the strategies, methods, and materials used to provide special education should be well-grounded in empirical research that substantiates their effectiveness. You understand how important this is if you have noticed the continuing cycle of unproven instructional fads and trendy practices in education.

Services provided *to* or *on behalf of* the student include:

- special education services
- related services
- supplementary aids and services

Services provided for *school personnel* include:

- program modifications
- supports

All of the provided services must help the student:

- advance appropriately toward attaining the annual goals,
- be involved in and make progress in the general education curriculum,
- participate in extracurricular and other nonacademic activities, and
- be educated and participate with other students with disabilities and nondisabled students in these activities.

Let's look at the services for students and school personnel.

• Special Education Services

What are special education services?
Special education services refer to *specially designed instruction* to meet the unique needs of students with disabilities as described in the annual goals. Specially designed instruction includes teaching, learning, practice, and assessment strategies that help students achieve annual goals, and may incorporate adaptations to the general curriculum.

Who receives special education services?
Students whose IEP annual goals require specially designed instruction receive special education services. Students may not receive special education services unless they have been classified with a disability and have a current IEP. IDEA states that children with disabilities are those who experience developmental delays (ages 3–9) or who are classified with one of these 12 disabilities:

- Autism
- Deaf-blindness
- Hearing impairment, including deafness
- Mental retardation

- Multiple disabilities
- Orthopedic impairment
- Other health impairment
- Serious emotional disturbance
- Specific learning disabilities
- Speech or language impairment
- Traumatic brain injury
- Visual impairment, including blindness

Your state may use different terms for some disability classifications, so be sure to learn your local terminology.

Who provides special education services?
Special education services are provided by or under the direction of licensed special educators. Special education paraeducators may also provide services to students with disabilities, but must do so under the direction of a licensed special educator.

Where are special education services provided?
Special education services are provided across a continuum of educational placements, including the regular class, a separate special education class, a separate special education facility, in the home, or in a hospital or other institution. It is important to understand that special education refers to services, not a certain place in the building. Therefore, a student in any of the above educational placements can receive special education services. The services provided and the locations of the services are determined by the IEP team within the requirements for LRE.

How do I write special education services on the IEP?
Here is an example of special education services for Brittany:

Special Education Services   R = *Regular class* S = *Special class* O = *Other* D = *Daily* W = *Weekly* M = *Monthly*

Service	Location	Time	Frequency	Begin date	Duration
Specially designed instruction	(R)(S) O:	*150 min*	(D) W M	*11/23*	(1 yr) O:

The IEP team has decided that the special education teacher will need to provide specially designed instruction to Brittany. She will teach Brittany replacement behaviors to eliminate her outbursts and refusal to work. This will occur in the resource room. The teacher will then reinforce desired behaviors while co-teaching in Brittany's regular classes. However, this level of detail is not required on the IEP form; the team only needs to note that Brittany will be provided specially designed instruction in both the regular class and in a special class.

• Related Services

What are related services?
Related services refer to transportation and developmental, corrective, and other supportive services needed to help a student with disabilities benefit from special education. Related services include:

- Counseling, including rehabilitation counseling
- Early identification and assessment of disabling conditions
- Interpreting services
- Medical services
- Orientation and mobility services
- Physical and occupational therapy
- Psychological services
- Recreation, including therapeutic recreation
- School nurse services
- Social work services
- Speech-language pathology and audiology services
- Transportation

Who receives related services?

Any student with an IEP may receive related services if they are necessary for the student to benefit from special education. For example, a student may receive specialized instruction for specific learning disabilities and also receive speech-language services. Another student may just receive orientation and mobility services, but not receive any other specially designed instruction.

Who provides related services?

Related services are provided by or under the direction of the various professionals licensed to provide the particular service. IEP teams commonly include a school psychologist, a speech-language pathologist, a physical therapist, or an occupational therapist, depending upon the needs of the student.

Where are related services provided?

Related services can be provided in a regular class, a separate room or office, or in an extra-curricular setting, depending upon the needs of the student.

How do I write related services on the IEP?

Here is the related services section from Isabel's IEP:

Related Services to Benefit from Special Education

Service	Location	Time	Frequency	Begin date	Duration
Speech-language services	R ⓢ O:	*60 min.*	D Ⓦ M	*4/21*	① yr O:

You will notice that Isabel's IEP specifies speech-language services to address her goals to improve articulation, to learn to ask for clarification when needed, and expressing her feelings to others.

• Supplementary Aids and Services

What are supplementary aids and services?

Supplementary aids and services are aids, services and other supports that are provided in regular education classes or other education-related settings to enable students with disabilities to be educated with nondisabled students to the maximum extent appropriate (notice the emphasis on LRE). Supplementary aids and services are provided when the IEP team determines that the student will need adjustments or modifications to the general curriculum or instruction in order to meet IEP goals.

When supplementary aids and services are needed, the IEP team may determine that teachers must make adjustments or modifications in one or more of the following areas:

- The ways teachers present information

  —A student with visual impairments may need large-print materials.

  —A student who is deaf and lip reads may need to see the teacher's face when he is speaking.

  —A student who cannot process sequential instructions well may need the teacher to model each of the steps and be provided with a step-by-step list to follow.

- The ways students complete tasks

  —A student who has poor motor skills may need to dictate written expression to a scribe.

  —A student who has difficulty grasping math concepts may need instruction with manipulative objects to learn new skills or concepts.

  —A student may require assistive technology for speaking, listening, reading, or writing.

- The ways teachers assess student learning

  —A student who processes information slowly may need more time to complete a test.

  —A student who attends school only in the afternoon because of a health impairment will need tests scheduled for that time.

  —A student who is highly distractible may need to be tested in a distraction-free environment.

  —A student who cannot read well or who has a visual impairment may need to have a test dictated.

  —A student who cannot speak may need to point to indicate answers to test items.

- The ways teachers structure the environment

  —A student who is easily distracted may need reduced-distraction seating or work areas, such as those away from windows, fish tanks, or open doors.

  —A student using a walker will need wide enough pathways to access all areas of the classroom.

  —A student who uses a wheelchair will need materials and equipment placed within reach.

  —A student with visual impairments will need a predictable and seldom-changed physical environment for ease of navigation in the classroom.

—A student who has hearing impairments will need visual access to any information that other students learn from hearing, such as the public address system or movies shown in class.

—A student who has difficulty learning and following classroom routines may benefit from a posted daily schedule to anticipate transitions between activities.

Who receives supplementary aids and services?

Any student with an IEP may receive supplementary aids and services if the services are necessary for the student to benefit from special education. For example, a student who cannot use a regular computer keyboard may need an adapted keyboard with larger keys. Another student may just require large-print materials, but not need any specially designed instruction.

Who provides supplementary aids and services?

Supplementary aids and services may be provided by a regular class teacher, a paraeducator, a special educator, a related service provider, or other qualified school personnel. The school administrator may provide a supplementary aid if it requires the purchase of equipment or alterations to the school facilities.

Where are supplementary aids and services provided?

Supplementary aids and services are provided in the regular class or other curricular or extra-curricular environments to meet the student's IEP goals. The primary focus of providing supplementary aids and services is to facilitate student success in the regular class and other environments with nondisabled peers.

How do I write supplementary aids and services on the IEP?

Here is the supplementary aids and services statement from Herbie's IEP:

Program Modifications and/or Supplementary Aids and Services in Regular Classes

Modifications/Personnel Support	Frequency	Supplementary Aids and Services	Frequency
	D W M	*Tests written at grade 1 reading level*	D ⓦ M

Herbie reads at about the 1st grade level, so this will help him access written tests in the general curriculum.

• Program Modifications or Supports

What are program modifications or supports?

Program modifications or supports assist teachers to meet unique and specific needs of students with disabilities. Let's briefly explore each of these terms.

- *Program modifications* include interventions and accommodations necessary for the teacher to help the student achieve IEP goals. An example is a student whose behavior interferes with learning and needs a program of positive behavioral supports in the school environment to learn more acceptable and productive behaviors. The IEP team would discuss these needs, describe the necessary modifications on the IEP, and provide the support needed to help the teacher implement the program.

- *Supports* include special training for teachers that help them meet unique or specific needs of students in the classroom. An example is training a teacher to enter new vocabulary words into a student's communication device so the student can use the new vocabulary as other students are assigned to do.

Who receives program modifications or supports?
School personnel who are responsible for addressing a student's goals receive program modifications or supports if they are noted on the IEP.

Who provides program modifications or supports?
Program modifications or supports can be provided to school personnel by a special educator, a paraeducator, a related service provider, a staff developer or another education professional.

Where are program modifications or supports provided?
Program modifications or supports can be provided in the regular class or other curricular or extra-curricular environments to meet the student's IEP goals. These modifications and supports should help the student achieve annual goals in the least restrictive environment.

How do I write program modifications or supports on the IEP?
Tabib's IEP includes this program support for his teachers:

Program Modifications and/or Supplementary Aids and Services in Regular Classes

Modifications/Personnel Support	Frequency	Supplementary Aids and Services	Frequency
Autism training and consultation	D W Ⓜ	*Personal communication device*	Ⓓ W M

Tabib's regular class teacher has never taught a child with autism, so the team has determined that a specialist in autism, augmentative communication, and behavioral issues will provide training and consultation to this teacher and to his special educator.

• Special Factors to Consider

Depending on the needs of the student, the IEP team must consider what IDEA calls *special factors.* Special factors include:

- If the student's **behavior** interferes with his or her learning or the learning of others, the IEP team will consider positive behavior interventions and supports to address the student's behavior.

- If the student has **limited proficiency in English,** the IEP team will consider the student's language needs as these needs relate to his or her IEP.

- If the student is **blind or visually impaired,** the IEP team must provide for instruction in Braille or the use of Braille, unless it determines after an appropriate evaluation that the student does not need this instruction.

- If the student has **communication** needs, the IEP team must consider those needs, and if the student is deaf or hard of hearing, the IEP team must consider his or her language and communication needs. This includes the student's opportunities to communicate directly with classmates and school staff in his or her usual method of communication (for example, sign language).

- The IEP team must consider the student's need for **assistive technology** devices or services.

How do I write special factors on the IEP?
Refer to Tabib's IEP. It indicates that he needs positive behavior instruction and support, communication and language services, and assistive technology.

How does the team decide what services the student needs?

The team considers the student's PLAAFP statements and annual goals and then decides the type of service that will best help the student achieve the goals. For example, if you look at Isabel's IEP, you will see that she has annual goals in math, language arts, social/emotional, communication, functional life skills, and career/vocational. The IEP team determined that a range of services for Isabel and her workplace manager are necessary to achieve the goals.

May I see examples of IEP team decisions for determining services?

Sure. Refer to the IEPs for our four students. You will see the services listed after the annual goals. This IEP format is a good reminder that teams set annual goals, and then decide which services are needed to meet those goals.

TIME FOR SOME PRACTICE.

Refer to Tabib's IEP and answer the following questions. Then compare your answers with our model in the Appendix.

1. *What special education services does Tabib require?* _____

2. *What related services does Tabib require?* _____

3. *What supplementary aids and services does Tabib require?* _____

4. *What program modifications and supports do Tabib's teachers require?* _____

5. *What special factors did the IEP team consider?* _____

6. Explain why you think the team recommended these services. _____

_____

_____

_____

_____

What decisions does the team make regarding the date, frequency, location, and duration of services to be provided?

Once the team decides what special education and related services are required, they record this information on the IEP and specify the following:

- **Date:** when the special education and related services will begin. The IEP is in effect when it is signed by the team but services may not begin until the next school day.

- **Frequency:** how often the services will be provided. The decision about frequency of services is made by the team as agreed upon by those who provide the services. Check with your school or district regarding whether they require time increments to be recorded in minutes or hours; daily, weekly, or monthly.

- **Location:** where the services will be provided. The team is required by IDEA to provide services in the least restrictive environment.

- **Duration:** the length of time the services will be provided. IDEA requires the team to review the IEP at least annually, but the team may review and/or rewrite the IEP more often if needed to meet the individual needs of the student.

These important aspects of the IEP provide specific information to parents, teachers, and students regarding the number and type of services the student will receive, and when and where those services will be provided. The IEP form will have a place to specify this information, perhaps similar to this table:

Special Education Services   *R = Regular class S = Special class O = Other D = Daily W = Weekly M = Monthly*

Service	Location	Time	Frequency	Begin date	Duration
	R S O:		D W M		1 yr O:
	R S O:		D W M		1 yr O:

Is there anything tricky to watch for at this stage of IEP development?

Yes, there is. A common error occurs when the team confuses the term "service" with the term "location." For example, it is incorrect for the team to write "special class" as a service. "Special class" is a *location*. The type of service would be specially designed instruction, or speech therapy, or life skills instruction, or some other such term.

May I see some examples of this part of IEP decision making?

Of course. Take a look at these:

- Herbie's goals are all academic and can best be achieved by providing daily specially designed instruction, so his service can be written as follows:

Special Education Services   R = *Regular class* S = *Special class* O = *Other* D = *Daily* W = *Weekly* M = *Monthly*

Service	Location	Time	Frequency	Begin date	Duration
Specially designed instruction	R (S) O:	*275 min*	D (W) M	*12/16*	(1 yr) O:

Note that the time is written as "minutes per week" because Herbie's school has a weekly early-out day to provide planning and teaming time for the teachers. His schedule in the resource room must be adjusted for that day, so instead of an hour each day, he receives a total of 275 minutes for the week.

- Tabib has many needs and his goals cover both academic achievement and functional performance. His services can be written like this:

Special Education Services   R = *Regular class* S = *Special class* O = *Other* D = *Daily* W = *Weekly* M = *Monthly*

Service	Location	Time	Frequency	Begin date	Duration
Specially designed instruction	R (S) O:	*3 hrs.*	(D) W M	*9/16*	(1 yr) O:
Specially designed instruction	(R) S O:	*3 hrs.*	(D) W M	*9/16*	(1 yr) O:

Related Services to Benefit from Special Education

Service	Location	Time	Frequency	Begin date	Duration
Speech-language services	R (S) O:	*45 min.*	(D) W M	*9/16*	(1 yr) O:

Program Modifications and/or Supplementary Aids and Services in Regular Classes

Modifications / Personnel Support	Frequency	Supplementary Aids and Services	Frequency
Autism training and consultation	D W (M)	*Personal communication device*	(D) W M

Applicable Special Factors

Factor	Not Needed	In IEP
Positive behavior instruction and support when behavior impedes learning of student or others		✔
Language needs for student with limited English proficiency	✔	
Braille instruction for student who is blind or visually impaired	✔	
Communication and/or language services for student who is deaf, hard of hearing, or has other communication needs		✔
Assistive technology devices or services		✔

Are there special considerations for providing services to secondary students with IEPs?

Yes. IDEA requires that IEP teams address **transition planning** for students age 16 and older. You will learn this important process in Step 7.

Let's summarize the requirements for this step.

1. Determine what services will be provided *to* or *on behalf of* the student, which may include
   - special education services
   - related services
   - supplementary aids and services

2. Determine what services will be provided for *school personnel,* which may include:
   - program modifications
   - supports

3. Make sure that all of the provided services will help the student:
   - advance appropriately toward attaining the annual goals,
   - be involved in and make progress in the general education curriculum,
   - participate in extracurricular and other nonacademic activities, and
   - be educated and participate with other students with disabilities and nondisabled students in these activities.

WHEW!
YOU'VE COMPLETED STEP 4, SO LET'S SEE WHAT HAPPENS IN **STEP 5.**

✔ Describe the student's present levels of academic achievement and functional performance.

✔ Write measurable annual goals.

✔ Measure and report student progress.

✔ State the services needed to achieve annual goals.

5️⃣ Explain the extent, if any, to which the student will not participate with nondisabled students in the regular class and in extracurricular and other nonacademic activities.

6️⃣ Explain accommodations necessary to measure academic achievement and functional performance on state and district-wide assessments.

7️⃣ Complete a transition plan for students aged 16 and older.

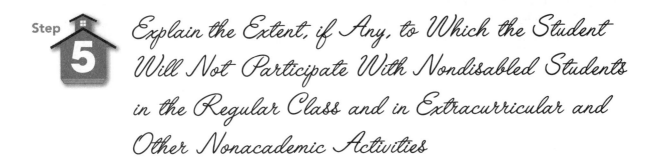

Explain the Extent, if Any, to Which the Student Will Not Participate With Nondisabled Students in the Regular Class and in Extracurricular and Other Nonacademic Activities

The law presumes that a student with disabilities will be involved in and make progress in the general education curriculum and participate with nondisabled students in the regular class, extracurricular and other nonacademic activities. In cases where a student will not participate, the IEP team must include a statement of the extent, if any, to which the student will not participate with nondisabled students in the regular class, extracurricular activities, and other nonacademic activities.

What are the concerns about excluding students with disabilities from the regular school program?

The concerns about excluding students from any aspect of the regular school program center on the tendency for such exclusion to result in lowered expectations. When students are restricted from regular classes and instruction they are often taught a different curriculum and held to different achievement standards, and therefore they perform poorly on tests that are based upon the general curriculum. When students are restricted from extracurricular or other nonacademic activities they miss out on important social interactions and opportunities to enrich their educational experiences.

What is meant by the terms "regular class, extracurricular activities, and other nonacademic activities?"

The following examples will help you understand what is meant by these terms.

- **The regular class**
  Typically, the regular class is where students receive instruction in grade-level appropriate curriculum with nondisabled peers. Students with disabilities are expected to participate in the regular class unless removed for instruction in a more restrictive setting.

- **Extracurricular activities**
  Extracurricular activities are supplementary to the general curriculum and are not required by state curriculum standards. These often vary from school to school and may include activities such as:
  —basketball

  —pep squad

  —safety patrol

  —school clubs

- **Nonacademic activities**

  Nonacademic activities are part of the school day, but are not directly related to mandated curriculum or extracurricular activities. These may include:

  —breakfast

  —lunch

  —recess

  —school assemblies

  —class parties

How does the IEP team determine if a student will not participate in some aspects of the school program?

If the IEP team obtains sufficient evidence that a student is not progressing in some aspect of the regular school program, even with appropriate supplementary aids and services, then the team may decide that the student will not participate. IEP teams must be cautious not to exclude a student from the regular school program based solely on the disability classification. Most students who receive special education services can participate in the regular school program with varying degrees of adaptation or accommodation.

How does the team address this decision on the IEP?

The IEP must include an explanation of the extent to which the student will not participate in the regular school program. You will need to learn what your district or state requires for this part of the IEP. The school or district IEP form may include a statement such as the following:

> The student will participate in the regular class, extracurricular and nonacademic activities except as noted above and listed here: ☐ _____

May I see what this looks like?

You certainly may. Take another look at Tabib's IEP. You will find the following statement under *Participation in Regular Class, Extracurricular and Nonacademic Activities:*

> The student will participate in the regular class, extracurricular and nonacademic activities except as noted above and listed here: ☒ *Tabib will not participate in lunch in the cafeteria at the same time as other students or in school assemblies.*

Looking at Tabib's PLAAFP statements you will see that he is extremely sensitive to noise and crowds of people. Knowing that these sensitivities adversely affect his behavior, and, in turn, affect his progress in the curriculum, the team made the decision to exempt him from noisy and crowded school activities. Remember the requirement for a free and appropriate public education in the least restrictive environment? Tabib's IEP team decided that because of the effects of his disability, these two school activities are not appropriate for him.

YOUR TURN!

Read each of the following vignettes and write what you would advise the IEP team regarding nonparticipation. When completed, compare your recommendations with those in the Appendix.

1. **Sam** was born with cerebral palsy, which limits his fine and gross motor movement.

   The student will participate in the regular class, extracurricular and nonacademic activities except as noted above and listed here: ☐ _____

2. **Bria** receives specially designed reading instruction in the resource room for 30 minutes daily.

   The student will participate in the regular class, extracurricular and nonacademic activities except as noted above and listed here: ☐ _____

3. **Yakov** receives specially designed behavior supports in all regular classes.

   The student will participate in the regular class, extracurricular and nonacademic activities except as noted above and listed here: ☐ _____

Let's summarize the extent of nonparticipation in the regular class and in extracurricular and other nonacademic activities.

1. Students with disabilities are expected to participate in the general curriculum to the maximum extent appropriate.

2. The three areas in which students with disabilities might participate are:
   - the regular class
   - extracurricular activities
   - nonacademic activities

3. The IEP must include a statement explaining the extent to which a student will not participate in the regular class, and in extracurricular and other nonacademic activities.

4. This statement can be made by listing specific classes or activities in which the student will not participate.

✔ Describe the student's present levels of academic achievement and functional performance.

✔ Write measurable annual goals.

✔ Measure and report student progress.

✔ State the services needed to achieve annual goals.

✔ Explain the extent, if any, to which the student will not participate with nondisabled students in the regular class and in extracurricular and other nonacademic activities.

6 Explain accommodations necessary to measure academic achievement and functional performance on state and district-wide assessments.

7 Complete a transition plan for students aged 16 and older.

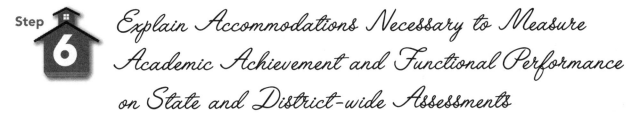

Step **6** *Explain Accommodations Necessary to Measure Academic Achievement and Functional Performance on State and District-wide Assessments*

In keeping with the principle of involvement and progress in the general education curriculum, students with disabilities are to participate with nondisabled students in State and district-wide assessments. Participation in these assessments assures that education professionals are accountable for the appropriate progress of all students. The law requires the IEP team to include a statement of any individual appropriate accommodations that are necessary to measure the academic achievement and functional performance of the child on State and district-wide assessments. If the team determines that a student with disabilities cannot reasonably participate in a particular State or district-wide assessment or part of an assessment, even with accommodations, then the team must select an alternate assessment in which the student will participate.

Notice that the law requires accommodations necessary to *measure academic achievement and functional performance.* This is more specific than the IDEA 1997 requirement for a statement of modifications needed for a student to participate in the assessment. IEP teams must now consider accurate measurement rather than just ways for the student to take part in the assessment.

How might students with disabilities participate in State or district-level assessments?

Students with disabilities can participate in State or district-level assessments under any of several conditions, based upon the IEP team's decision. Not all states offer all assessment options, so you need to check your state regulations to learn which options are available. Generally, the following assessment options are available for students with disabilities:

1. Regular assessment of grade-level academic content standards based on grade-level academic achievement standards

2. Regular assessment of grade-level academic content standards, with appropriate *accommodations,* based on grade-level academic achievement standards

3. Alternate assessment of grade-level academic content standards based on grade-level academic achievement standards

4. Alternate assessment of grade-level academic content standards based on *alternate* academic achievement standards

This table further illustrates these options:

	Regular Assessment	Regular Assessment with Accommodations	Alternate Assessment based on Grade-Level Achievement Standards	Alternate Assessment based on Alternate Achievement Standards
Content standards taught and assessed	Grade level	Grade level	Grade level	Grade level, with reduced complexity, depth, and/or breadth
Achievement standards	Grade level	Grade level	Grade level	Alternate standards
Participating students	Most students with disabilities (without accommodations)	Most students with disabilities (with accommodations)	Students with disabilities who need alternate ways to demonstrate their knowledge	Students with the most significant cognitive disabilities

Adapted from the version presented by Martha L. Thurlow during the Alternate Assessment Strand at the CEC Convention in Salt Lake City, Utah in February 2006, which was based on a table developed by R. Quenemoen for use in national technical assistance efforts, Spring 2005.

When are students with disabilities assessed on state and district-wide assessments?

Students with disabilities are tested on the same schedule as those without disabilities. Federal law requires the systematic assessment of student progress in specified grades for certain subjects (e.g., language arts, math, or science); however, your school district might require additional tests. Be sure to check with your school or district regarding the scheduling of State and district-wide assessments.

NOW LET'S LEARN HOW TO MAKE IEP DECISIONS FOR EACH OF THESE OPTIONS.

1. **What is regular assessment of grade-level academic content standards based on grade-level academic achievement standards?**

   This refers to students with disabilities taking the same tests under the same conditions as students without disabilities.

   - *How does the team decide that a student will participate in this type of testing?*

     The IEP team may decide that a student with a disability who has performed at capacity on previous assessments will take the same tests under the same conditions as students without disabilities. This decision must be made with ample evidence that taking the tests under standardized conditions does not prevent the student from demonstrating competency on the tests.

2. **What is regular assessment of grade-level academic content standards, with appropriate accommodations, based on grade-level academic achievement standards?**

   This means that students with disabilities take the same tests as students without disabilities, but under different conditions. It is important to remember that participating with accommodations means there are no changes to test content or administration *that fundamentally alter or lower the standard or expectations of the assessment.*

   - *How does the team decide that a student will participate in this type of testing?*

     The team should look at whether or not the student requires accommodations for classroom instruction and tests. If accommodations are required in the course of daily learning and classroom assessments, then the student will most likely require the same or similar accommodations for State and district-wide assessments, depending on the content being assessed.

   - *How does the team select appropriate accommodations for state and district-wide assessments?*

     The team can select appropriate accommodations based on answers to these or similar questions:

     — What accommodations is the student regularly using in the classroom and on classroom tests of content similar to what is covered on the State or district wide assessment?

     — What is the student's perception of how well an accommodation has worked?

     — Has the student been willing to use the accommodation?

     — What is the evidence from parents, teachers, and others about how the accommodations have worked?

     — Have there been difficulties administering the selected accommodations? (National Center for Learning Disabilities, 2005). While the difficulty of providing specific accommodations should not warrant their removal, IEP teams may select different accommodations which are equally effective, but not as intrusive or difficult to administer.

   - *What are some examples of assessment accommodations?*

     Let's look at some examples here. Please remember that with accommodations the content and administration of the test *is not* fundamentally changed in ways that alter or lower the standard or expectations of the assessment. Be sure to check the State or district guidelines regarding which accommodations are acceptable without fundamentally altering or lowering the academic achievement standard of the test. Here are several examples of accommodations for various test administration domains:

Setting

— provide a distraction-free environment such as a study carrel

— provide special furniture, such as an adjustable-height desk for a wheelchair

— provide a small-group setting

Scheduling

— provide extended testing time within the same day

— administer the test in several sessions within total time allowance

Test format

— provide Braille edition

— present test in student's native language

— increase spacing, fewer items per page, or only one sentence per line

— provide magnification or amplification equipment

Test directions

— read directions to student

— provide recorded directions

— simplify language to clarify or explain

— repeat directions for subtasks

Test procedures

— read content aloud, except for reading subtests where specific skills being assessed preclude reading aloud.

— use sign language for orally presented test items

— provide written copies of orally presented materials that are found only in administrator's manual

Student response format

— allow students to mark answer in test booklet rather than transfer to bubble sheet

— permit student to answer by pointing, signing, typing, orally responding, or other non-written response

— audio record student's responses

— provide template or placeholder for answer document

May I see an example of selected accommodations on an IEP?

Sure. Let's refer to Herbie's IEP. Notice that his PLAAFP statements indicate that he has limited reading ability, and his IEP lists "tests written at grade 1 reading level" under *Supplementary Aids and Services.* Correspondingly, the team wrote "read test to student" as an accommodation, except for tests or subtests that specifically measure subskills of reading achievement that preclude reading aloud.

PRACTICE
CHOOSING APPROPRIATE
ACCOMMODATIONS
FOR THESE STUDENTS.

Read each of the following cases and write your suggestions for appropriate accommodations for State and district-wide assessments. Then compare your answers with our suggestions in the Appendix.

- Bernadette has fine motor limitations which prevent her from holding or using a pencil.

  Suggested accommodation: _____

- Felipe has visual impairments that prevent him from reading normally-sized print.

  Suggested accommodation: _____

- DeShane's attention deficit disorder significantly impairs his ability to concentrate in groups larger than three or four students.

  Suggested accommodation: _____

3. What is alternate assessment of grade-level academic content standards based on grade-level academic achievement standards?

An alternate assessment of grade-level content standards based on grade-level achievement standards addresses the same content and holds students to the same expectations as does the regular grade-level test, but students participate in some other way than the usual paper and pencil test. For example, students may demonstrate content mastery through work samples aligned with the grade-level standards. IEP teams must be cautious in selecting the alternate means by which students will demonstrate their skills, because these alternate tests must be determined to be comparable to the regular assessment, as well as valid and reliable in order to be eligible for determining test scores that contribute to accountability calculations. For purposes of the *No Child Left Behind Act* (NCLB), these standards of comparability to the regular assessment are very high.

- *How does the team decide that a student will participate in this type of testing?*

  Similar to determining appropriate accommodations, the team would consider the ways in which the student successfully demonstrates learning in the classroom on comparable content. If sufficient evidence exists to show that the student more accurately demonstrates achievement or ability in an alternate way, then the IEP team may choose this option.

4. What is alternate assessment of grade-level academic content standards based on alternate academic achievement standards?

An alternate assessment based on alternate achievement standards that is linked to grade level content standards, but with reduced complexity, depth, or breadth. These tests reflect an alternate level of expectations in the areas of reading/language arts, mathematics, and science than do regular assessments or alternate assessments based on grade-level achievement standards. In general, alternate achievement standards must be aligned with a State's academic content standards, promote access to the general curriculum, and reflect professional judgment of the highest achievement standards possible.

- *How does the team decide that a student will participate in this type of testing?*

  The team decides by considering guidelines for why a student would participate in this type of testing rather than in the standard state or district-wide testing. Guidelines might include the following:

  A student with a significant cognitive disability

  1. who requires substantial modifications, adaptations, or supports to meaningfully access the grade-level content,

  2. who requires intensive individualized instruction in order to acquire and generalize knowledge, and

  3. who is unable to demonstrate achievement of academic content standards on a paper and pencil test, even with accommodations.

- *What must be included on the IEP if a student takes an alternate assessment?*

  If the team determines that a student with disabilities cannot reasonably participate in a particular State or district-wide assessment or part of an assessment, even with accommodations, then the team must select an alternate assessment in which the student will participate. The IEP must include a statement explaining:

  —why the student cannot participate in the regular assessment, and

  —why the particular alternate assessment selected is appropriate for the student.

- *What alternate assessments can the team select?*

  IEP teams are given authority to administer alternate assessments appropriate for measuring students' academic achievement and functional performance. However, the types of assessments from which these teams can choose depends upon individual state or district regulations. Generally, the types of assessments available include checklists, portfolios, and task performance demonstrations, including the use of assistive technology. These assessments must have an explicit structure and have clearly delineated scoring criteria and procedures. They also should be valid, reliable, accessible, objective, and consistent with nationally recognized professional and technical standards. Be sure to check with your school district regarding alternate assessment options in your state.

May I see an example of this statement?

Of course. Take a look at Tabib's IEP and you will see the following statements:

Alternate Assessment

State why student cannot participate in regular assessment: *Tabib requires substantial modifications to meaningfully access the grade-level content and requires intensive individualized instruction in order to acquire and generalize knowledge.*

State why selected alternate assessment is appropriate: *The selected alternate assessment aligns with the substantial modifications and intensive individualized instruction necessary for Tabib to acquire and generalize grade-level knowledge.*

> LET'S PRACTICE CHOOSING APPROPRIATE ALTERNATE ASSESSMENTS.

Read each of the following cases and write your suggestions for alternate assessment. Compare your answers with our suggestions in the Appendix.

- Absalom requires substantial adaptations and supports to meaningfully access the grade-level content, requires intensive individualized instruction to acquire and generalize knowledge, and is unable to demonstrate achievement of academic content standards on a paper and pencil test, even with accommodations.

  Suggested testing: _____

- LaTasha's significant cognitive disability and orthopedic impairments prevent her from successfully participating in standardized assessments, even with accommodations and modifications.

  Suggested testing: _____

Let's summarize how the team explains necessary accommodations for state and district-wide assessments.

The team considers the students strengths, needs, and abilities, and then chooses one of these options, as allowed by the particular state, and plans accordingly:

1. Regular assessment of grade-level academic content standards based on grade-level academic achievement standards

2. Regular assessment of grade level academic content standards, with appropriate *accommodations,* based on grade-level academic achievement standards

3. Alternate assessment of grade-level academic content standards based on grade-level academic achievement standards

4. Alternate assessment of grade-level academic content standards based on *alternate* academic achievement standards

References

National Center for Learning Disabilities. (2005). *No Child Left Behind: Determining appropriate assessment accommodations for students with disabilities.* New York: Author. Available at http://www.ncld.org/content/view/284/322/

Kearns, J. & Browder, D. (2006, April). *1% and 2%: All for learning! What do we know?* Presentation at the Council for Exceptional Children Conference in Salt Lake City, Utah.

✔ Describe the student's present levels of academic achievement and functional performance.

✔ Write measurable annual goals.

✔ Measure and report student progress.

✔ State the services needed to achieve annual goals.

✔ Explain the extent, if any, to which the student will not participate with nondisabled students in the regular class and in extracurricular and other nonacademic activities.

✔ Explain accommodations necessary to measure academic achievement and functional performance on state and district-wide assessments.

7 Complete a transition plan for students aged 16 and older.

Step

7

Complete a Transition Plan for Students Aged 16 and Older

Beginning not later than the first IEP to be in effect when the student turns 16, or younger if determined appropriate by the IEP team, and updated annually, thereafter, the IEP must include:

- Appropriate measurable postsecondary goals based upon age-appropriate transition assessments related to training, education, employment, and, where appropriate, independent living skills; and

- The transition services (including courses of study) needed to assist the student in reaching those goals.

- Transfer of rights at the age of majority. Beginning not later than one year before the student reaches the age of majority under State law, the IEP must include a statement that the student has been informed of the student's rights under Part B of the Act, if any, that will transfer to the student on reaching the age of majority.

What is transition planning?

Transition planning is a student-centered process of structuring course work and other educational experiences to prepare the student for transition from school to adult life. Transition planning results in a formal document that is individualized to the needs and aspirations of the student for adult living.

Does transition planning ever apply to students younger than 16?

Yes. The IEP team may begin transition planning and services at an earlier age if the effects of the student's disability are such that more time is required to prepare for transition to adult life.

What are the requirements for transition planning?

The transition plan must include these elements:

- Appropriate measurable postsecondary goals based upon age-appropriate transition assessments related to
    —training
    —education
    —employment
    —and, where appropriate, independent living skills,

- Transition services, including courses of study, necessary to assist the student in reaching the goals,

- A statement that the student has been informed of transfer of adult rights not later than one year before the student reaches the age of majority.

How does the team accomplish transition planning?

Let's answer this question by explaining how the team addresses each of the three elements.

1. *Measurable postsecondary goals*

   The first step in transition planning is for the student, in conjunction with the IEP team, to explore aspirations for the student's future. The law requires the goals to be based on data from appropriate transition assessments. This is best accomplished when the IEP team and representatives of community agencies that may provide transition services use assessment results to guide discussion of the student's career interests, desires for continuing education, and expectations for independent adult living. The student's interests are then translated into postsecondary goals in four areas:

   - **Education.** Goals for education include what the student wants to study in a post-secondary setting, where the student wants to study, what is required for admission to the desired school and program, and the associated financial obligations.

   - **Training.** Training refers to specific skills necessary for desired employment such as word processing, equipment operation, food handling, interpersonal relations, or carpentry.

   - **Employment.** Goals for employment focus on the student's desired trade or occupation. The target occupation may be available to the student immediately upon high school graduation or may require specific training or education.

   - **Independent living.** Goals in this area relate to the type of housing the student desires upon completion of school as well as transportation necessary to access community services and activities.

   - **Daily living skills.** Goals in this area include personal living skills such as cooking, eating, dressing, and grooming.

2. *Transition services, including courses of study, necessary to assist the student in reaching the goals*

   The second step in transition planning is determine what services must be provided during the school years to help the student reach the postsecondary goals. Because transition services may be provided outside the school, the team must invite a representative of any participating agency that is likely to be responsible for providing or paying for transition services. Such agencies may include public or private job training services, welfare services, mental health agencies, or other community-based programs.

   Transition services may include any or all of the following:

   - **Instruction,** including courses of study that address academic or skill-training preparation for achieving postsecondary goals.

   - **Related services** necessary for the student to achieve annual goals.

   - **Community experiences** provided outside the school, including community-based job exploration, job site training, banking, shopping, transportation, health care, counseling, and recreation activities.

   - If appropriate, the acquisition of **daily living skills,** such as grooming, laundry care, food preparation, and budgeting.

- If appropriate, the provision of a **functional vocational evaluation** to determine the student's readiness for employment. This involves a comprehensive assessment of the student's vocational preferences and skills to work in both general and specific work settings. The evaluation can be accomplished with formal or informal assessments of the student's strengths, aptitudes, interests, work experiences, and other relevant attributes.

3. *A statement that the student has been informed of the transfer of adult rights no later than one year before the student reaches the age of majority*

   The third requirement for transition planning is to inform the student of the pending transfer of adult rights, if any, to the student at the age of legal adult status in the state of residence. This requirement must be completed no later than *one year before* the student reaches the age of majority. Check with your local school or district to see if a special form is used for this process.

May I see an example of a transition plan?

Most assuredly. Look back at Isabel's transition plan in the *Meet Our Students* section. You will find each requirement addressed on the form. Note that the IEP and the Transition Plan are complementary documents and that IEP teams serve secondary students most effectively when IEP goals are addressed with educational services as well as community-based services.

Select the service(s) your IEP team would recommend for Charlotte, a 17-year-old girl with orthopedic impairments, in order to meet the annual goal listed below. Check your answers with our suggestions in the Appendix.

Annual Goal

When Charlotte arrives at work from the city bus, she will independently wheel herself into the building, clock in, and begin her work, with no verbal prompts, for at least 4 weeks.

Services:

☐ Training

☐ Education

☐ Employment

☐ Independent Living

☐ Daily Living Skills

CONGRATULATIONS!
YOU HAVE LEARNED
ALL SEVEN STEPS
FOR WRITING
QUALITY IEPs!

Now you should be ready to serve on a team of parents and professionals who are committed to serving all students with disabilities in an ethical and professional manner. If you want to practice writing a complete IEP and Transition Plan, we have included sample blank forms in the Appendix. Remember, your state or district forms may look different, but they will have all of the seven steps that you have just mastered. Seven steps, that's all! You can be a master of writing quality IEPs!

Appendix

STEP 1

PLAAFP for Samuel (p. 44)

Samuel adds and subtracts one-digit addition and subtraction with no renaming, 9/10 correct; 2-digit/1-digit without renaming, 0/10 correct; 0/5 multiplication and division correct. He cannot multiply or divide. He dictates, but cannot compose and write simple sentences when given a concrete subject. He correctly identifies his backpack, but does not place school materials in the backpack when directed. He uses the restroom independently, but does not zip pants or wash hands before leaving restroom. He follows 2-step requests in order, but he does not wait his turn in line; he talks with his friends, but interrupts others in their conversations. Samuel's difficulties with math, written language, and self-help and socialization skills inhibit his progress in the academic and social curriculum.

Error in Lance's PLAAFP (p. 45)

This statement only provides some of Lance's strengths with no logical cues for writing annual goals. A more specific statement would require additional information related to this skill, such as, "Lance initiates and sustains conversations with peers and can call his friends on the telephone. He does not ask his teacher for assistance when needed. He makes inappropriate or unwanted sexual comments to female peers. Lance's communication deficits inhibit his progress in the general language curriculum."

Error in Nathan's PLAAFP (p. 45)

This statement provides information which is not related to Nathan's disability, which is in reading, not penmanship. A better statement would require specific information about Nathan's reading skills, such as, "Nathan can decode consonant-vowel-consonant (CVC) words and can read primer-level sentences. Nathan does not decode one- or two-syllable words with or without common endings, and reads 1.0 grade-level passages at less than 15 words correct per minute. Nathan's reading deficits inhibit his progress in the general reading curriculum."

Error in Corina's PLAAFP (p. 45)

This statement provides a vague description of Corina's social/behavioral skills. A more descriptive PLAAFP would require specific information about her social/behavioral skills, such as, "When directed to engage in work-related tasks, Corina throws her school materials and yells at the teacher an average of 8 times per day. She complains daily that she does not like school. Corina's behavior interferes with her progress in the general academic and social curriculum."

STEP 2

Annual Goal for Jessica (p. 52)

Conditions: When given a grocery list with 5 or fewer items and a $10.00 bill

Behavior: Jessica will select and purchase

Criteria: all the items on the list with fewer than 5 prompts

Generalization: in 3 different grocery stores

Maintenance: over a three-week period

Example of an Annual Goal for Morris (p. 52)

Conditions: When directed by the teacher to be seated

Behavior: Morris will quietly sit at his desk

Criteria: within 5 seconds, 90% of instances

Generalization: in each of his classes

Maintenance: over a 4-week period.

Benchmarks for Noah's Annual Goal (p. 56)

When presented with 10 items and asked to count them, Noah will point to and orally count the items correctly with no prompts.

Level of Assistance

1. *Benchmark:* In 10 weeks, when presented with 10 items and asked to count them, Noah will point to and orally count the items correctly with **verbal prompts,** 10/10 correct.

2. *Benchmark:* In 15 weeks, when presented with 10 items and asked to count them, Noah will point to and orally count the items correctly with **no prompts,** 10/10 correct.

Task Analysis

1. *Benchmark:* In 10 weeks, when presented with **5 items** and asked to count them, Noah will point to and orally count the items correctly with no prompts, 5/5 correct.

2. *Benchmark:* In 10 weeks, when presented with **10 items** and asked to count them, Noah will point to and orally count the items correctly with no prompts, 10/10 correct.

Generalization

1. *Benchmark:* In 10 weeks, when presented with 10 **identical** items and asked to count them, Noah will point to and orally count the items correctly with no prompts, 10/10 correct.

2. *Benchmark:* In 10 weeks, when presented with 10 **dissimilar** items and asked to count them, Noah will point to and orally count the items correctly with no prompts, 10/10 correct.

Short-term Objectives for Noah's Goal (p. 57)

1. *Short-term objective:* When presented with 10 items and asked to point to each, Noah will point to each item, 10/10 correct, 3/3 consecutive trials.

2. *Short-term objective:* When presented with 10 items and asked to point to and orally count them, Noah will point to and orally count all items, 10/10 correct, 3/3 consecutive trials.

STEP 3

Jamal's Annual Goal (p. 61)

When presented with 20 items of clothing, Jamal will correctly sort the clothing in preparation for laundering, once weekly for 3 consecutive weeks.

Measurement method: Teacher observation checklist

Reason: The teacher observation checklist allows the teacher to track progress as the student demonstrates mastery of each component of the skill.

Bentley's Annual Goal (p. 61)

When given 15 items of each type, Bentley will add and subtract single-digit items and write answers with no errors.

Measurement method: Curriculum-based measurement

Reason: The criteria require Bentley to write answers, so a test with 15 items for each operation is most appropriate.

STEP 4

Services for Tabib (pp. 73–74)

1. *What special education services does Tabib require?*
   - Specially designed instruction in the regular class and in the special education class.

2. *What related services does Tabib require?*
   - Speech-language services

3. *What supplementary aids and services does Tabib require?*
   - A personal communication device

4. *What program modifications and supports do Tabib's teachers require?*
   - Autism training and consultation

5. *What special factors did the IEP team consider?*
   - The IEP team considered Tabib's communication needs and his need for assistive technology to aid communication. These are listed above as supplementary aids and services. They also considered positive behavior instruction, as noted in his IEP goal.

6. *Explain why you recommend these services.*
   - Tabib needs specially designed instruction to address his goals, particularly as related to social, communication, behavior, and functional life skills. Also, since Tabib is in the 1st grade and has only five spoken words, it is imperative that he receive speech and language services and be provided with augmentative communication strategies or devices, such as sign language or a communication device. His regular class teacher has never taught a child with autism, so a specialist in autism, augmentative communication, and behavioral issues provide training and consultation to this teacher and to his special educator.

STEP 5

Statement of Nonparticipation (p. 79)

Sam was born with cerebral palsy which limits his fine and gross motor movement.

Our recommendation for Sam:

The student will participate in the regular class, extracurricular and nonacademic activities except as noted above and listed here: ☒ *Regular P.E.*

Sam will receive physical therapy and adaptive P.E. during the regular P.E. time.

Bria receives specially designed reading instruction in the resource room for 30 minutes daily.

Our recommendation for Bria:

The student will participate in the regular class, extracurricular and nonacademic activities except as noted above and listed here: ☒ *Reading instruction in the resource room*

Yakov receives specially designed behavior supports in all regular classes.

Our recommendation for Yakov:

The student will participate in the regular class, extracurricular and nonacademic activities except as noted above and listed here: ☐ *Not applicable*

STEP 6

Choosing Appropriate Accommodations (p. 85)

These accommodations are examples of what might be appropriate. Other options exist.

Bernadette has fine motor limitations which prevent her from holding or using a pencil.

Suggested accommodation: *dictate answers to scribe.*

Felipe has visual impairments that prevent him from reading normally sized print on a reading test.

Suggested accommodation: *provide large print materials or provide magnification equipment.*

DeShane's attention deficit disorder significantly impairs his ability to concentrate in groups larger than three or four students.

Suggested accommodation: *take test in study carrel or take test in room with 3 or fewer students.*

Choosing Appropriate Modifications (p. 87)

Jimmy's visual impairment prevents him from reading print on a reading test, but he has good listening comprehension skills.

Suggested modification: *teacher reads aloud reading subtests, student answers comprehension questions orally.*

Robyn cannot calculate math problems with paper and pencil, but can solve for problems by counting objects.

Suggested modification: *use manipulative objects for math subtests.*

Jemima has a health impairment that significantly reduces the amount of time she can work without resting.

Suggested modification: *provide more breaks than allowed by test publisher, or reduce number of test items.*

Choosing Alternate Assessments (p. 89)

Absalom requires substantial adaptations and supports to meaningfully access the grade-level content, requires intensive individualized instruction to acquire and generalize knowledge, and is unable to demonstrate achievement of academic content standards on a paper and pencil test, even with accommodations.

Suggested testing: *alternate assessment*

LaTasha's significant cognitive disability and orthopedic impairments prevent her from successfully participating in standardized assessments, even with accommodations and modifications.

Suggested testing: *alternate assessment*

STEP 7

Charlotte's Transition Plan (p. 93)

Services:

☒ Training—Charlotte may need training in order to achieve this goal.

☐ Education—This is a job-related goal, and post-secondary education is not mentioned.

☒ Employment—Charlotte needs a job in order to achieve this goal

☒ Independent Living—Charlotte needs transportation to get to her work site

☐ Daily Living Skills—This is a job-related goal; daily living skills are not mentioned.

INDIVIDUALIZED EDUCATION PROGRAM

Student _____ Birth date _____ IEP Date _____

School _____ Grade _____ Classification _____

Present Levels of Academic Achievement and Functional Performance

Preschool students: Describe how the disability affects the student's participation in appropriate activities.

School-age students: Describe how the disability affects the student's involvement and progress in the general curriculum.

_____

_____

_____

_____

_____

_____

Measurable Annual Goals

1. _____

_____

Student's progress toward goal measured by: ☐ Curriculum-based Measures ☐ Behavior Observation
☐ Skills Checklist ☐ Work Sample ☐ Test Results ☐ Other _____

2. _____

_____

Student's progress toward goal measured by: ☐ Curriculum-based Measures ☐ Behavior Observation
☐ Skills Checklist ☐ Work Sample ☐ Test Results ☐ Other _____

3. _____

_____

Student's progress toward goal measured by: ☐ Curriculum-based Measures ☐ Behavior Observation
☐ Skills Checklist ☐ Work Sample ☐ Test Results ☐ Other _____

4. _____

_____

Student's progress toward goal measured by: ☐ Curriculum-based Measures ☐ Behavior Observation
☐ Skills Checklist ☐ Work Sample ☐ Test Results ☐ Other _____

5. _____

_____

Student's progress toward goal measured by: ☐ Curriculum-based Measures ☐ Behavior Observation
☐ Skills Checklist ☐ Work Sample ☐ Test Results ☐ Other _____

6. _____

_____

Student's progress toward goal measured by: ☐ Curriculum-based Measures ☐ Behavior Observation
☐ Skills Checklist ☐ Work Sample ☐ Test Results ☐ Other _____

Services to Achieve Annual Goals and Advance in General Curriculum

Special Education Services   R = *Regular class* S = *Special class* O = *Other* D = *Daily* W = *Weekly* M = *Monthly*

Service	Location	Time	Frequency	Begin date	Duration
	R S O:		D W M		1 yr O:
	R S O:		D W M		1 yr O:
	R S O:		D W M		1 yr O:
	R S O:		D W M		1 yr O:

Related Services to Benefit from Special Education

Service	Location	Time	Frequency	Begin date	Duration
	R S O:		D W M		1 yr O:
	R S O:		D W M		1 yr O:
	R S O:		D W M		1 yr O:
	R S O:		D W M		1 yr O:

Program Modifications and/or Supplementary Aids and Services in Regular Classes

Modifications/Personnel Support	Frequency	Supplementary Aids and Services	Frequency
	D W M		D W M
	D W M		D W M
	D W M		D W M
	D W M		D W M

Applicable Special Factors

Factor	Not Needed	In IEP
Positive behavior instruction and support when behavior impedes learning of student or others		
Language needs for student with limited English proficiency		
Braille instruction for student who is blind or visually impaired		
Communication and/or language services for student who is deaf, hard of hearing, or has other communication needs		
Assistive technology devices or services		

Participation in Regular Class, Extracurricular and Nonacademic Activities

The student will participate in the regular class, extracurricular and nonacademic activities except as noted above and listed here: ☐ _____

Schedule for Written IEP Progress Reports to Parents

☐ Weekly   ☐ Bi-weekly ⎤
                              ⎥ *via* ⎡ ☐ Progress report   ☐ Report card
☐ Monthly   ☐ Quarterly ⎦   ⎣ ☐ Home note   ☐ Parent Conference

Transition Plan

Complete and attach for students age 16 and older.

Participation in State and District Assessments

Participation Codes

S	Standard administration	No accommodations or modifications
A	Participate with accommodations	Does not invalidate, alter, or lower standard
M	Participate with modifications	Invalidates, alters, or lowers standard
AA	Participate using alternate assessment: ☐ Out-of-level CRT ☐ State alternate assessment	Aligned more closely with alternate curriculum than general education curriculum

State and District Assessment Matrix   Enter appropriate participation code for each applicable assessment.

Grade	Kindergarten Pretest	Kindergarten Posttest	State Criterion Referenced Math	State Criterion Referenced Language Arts	State Criterion Referenced Science	Iowa Test of Basic Skills	National Assessment Educational Progress
K							
1							
2							
3							
4							
5							
6							
7							
8							
9							
10							
11							
12							

Accommodations and Modifications   List specific accommodations and modifications for assessments.

_____

_____

_____

Alternate Assessment

State why student cannot participate in regular assessment: _____

_____

_____

State why selected alternate assessment is appropriate: _____

_____

_____

_____

Student _____ Date _____

IEP Team Participants

_____ Parent

_____ LEA Representative

_____ Student

_____ Regular Class Teacher

_____ Special Education Teacher

_____ School Psychologist

_____ _____

_____ _____

If parent signature missing, provide copy of IEP and Procedural Safeguards and check below:

☐ Did not attend (document efforts to involve parent)

☐ Via telephone

☐ Other _____

Comments

TRANSITION PLAN

Student _____ Birth date _____ IEP Date _____

Transition Goals, Activities, and Services

Write the transition activities and services needed to achieve postsecondary goals. Refer to IEP goals or explain how transition activities/services will be provided. Indicate who is responsible and why services may not be needed.

1. Functional Vocational Evaluation.

Services needed to achieve goals	Agency responsible
Administer functional vocational evaluation	

OR indicate why service is not needed:
- ☐ Student functions independently in work settings.
- ☐ Other: _____

2. Education. See IEP goal(s) # _____ , or indicate here:
- ☐ Graduate with a regular diploma   ☐ Post-secondary education
- ☐ Graduate with a certificate of completion   ☐ Other: _____

Services needed to achieve goals	Agency responsible

3. Training. See IEP goal(s) # _____ , or list here:

Skill training goals:
Job training goals:

Services needed to achieve goals	Agency responsible

OR indicate why service is not needed:
- ☐ Student functions independently in work settings.
- ☐ Other: _____

4. Employment. See IEP goal(s) # _____ , or list here:

Services needed to achieve goals	Agency responsible

OR indicate why service is not needed:
- ☐ Student functions independently in work settings.
- ☐ Other: _____

5. **Independent Living.** See IEP goal(s) # _____ , or indicate here:

Housing
- ☐ Skilled Care Facility
- ☐ Group Home
- ☐ Supervised Apartment
- ☐ Supported Living
- ☐ Family home
- ☐ Apartment
- ☐ Home of own
- ☐ Other: _____

Transportation
- ☐ Independent transportation (e.g., walk, bicycle, car)
- ☐ Public transportation (e.g., bus, train)
- ☐ Specialized transportation
- ☐ Other: _____

Services needed to achieve goals	Agency responsible

OR indicate why service is not needed:
- ☐ Student functions independently.
- ☐ Other: _____

6. **Daily Living Skills, if appropriate.** See IEP goal(s) # _____ , or list here:

Services needed to achieve goals	Agency responsible

OR indicate why service is not needed:
- ☐ Student functions independently in work settings.
- ☐ Other: _____

Age of Majority

On or before the student's 17th birthday, inform the student and parent(s) of transfer of rights at age 18. See attached form, if applicable.

Nonparticipation in Transition Planning

If the student did not participate in this plan, indicate the steps taken to ensure the student's preferences were considered: _____

If a representative of an agency responsible for providing an activity did not participate, indicate the steps that will be taken to obtain the participation of the agency: _____